Design Technology

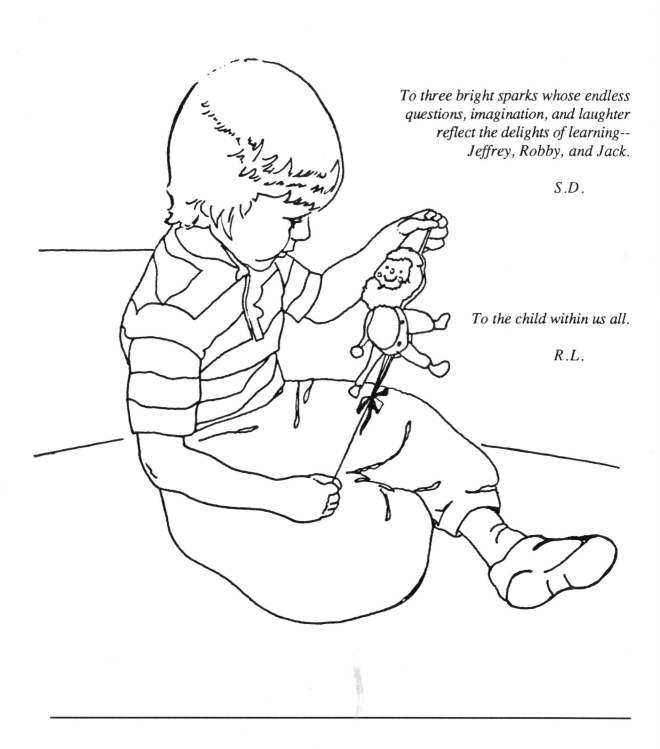

To three bright sparks whose endless questions, imagination, and laughter reflect the delights of learning-- Jeffrey, Robby, and Jack.

S.D.

To the child within us all.

R.L.

Design Technology
Children's Engineering

Susan Dunn

Gladstone School District

Rob Larson

Oregon Museum of Science and Industry

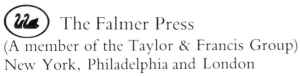 The Falmer Press
(A member of the Taylor & Francis Group)
New York, Philadelphia and London

UK   The Falmer Press, Falmer House, Barcombe,
        Lewes, East Sussex, BN8 5DL

USA   The Falmer Press, Taylor & Francis Inc.,
        1900 Frost Road, Suite 101, Bristol PA 19007

First published in 1990.
Printed in Hong Kong by Imago

CIP and LoC data available on request.

ISBN: 1-85000-590-7

Page and cover design by Susan Dunn and Rob Larson
Graphic work by Susan Dunn

Contents

Foreword

Design Technology: Children's Engineering draws on a long tradition of educational thought going back to John Locke, Jean-Jacques Rousseau, and a series of British educational reports dating as early as 1882. Americans can best understand children's engineering by linking it with the best of the American progressive educational tradition. It is the tough-minded, realistic, humane progressivism of John Dewey and his soundest interpreters.

This book presents a grassroots, child-centered approach to true educational transformation. Educators may see this as part of a new progressivism which includes such elements as cooperative learning, the whole language approach to literacy, and inquiry-based approaches in science and math. Children working with design technology have rich experiences which empower them to shape their environment, to develop their own evaluation skills, and to integrate concepts and skills from diverse curriculum areas. They learn to use their minds and hands interactively, to work collaboratively with other students, and to reflect thoughtfully about the processes used and the products which result. Children reflect orally and in writing as they consider materials and develop problem-solving skills which help them to deal more effectively with future challenges.

Design technology will not be the last word in education. But, it will be one more step in an honorable tradition which seeks to help children and teachers work together for educational and social improvement.

I can make no stronger case for this book than to apply to it the statement which John Dewey made nearly half a century ago in his introduction to Agnes de Lima's *The Little Red School House*. Dewey wrote that the book made "a deeply serious claim upon the attention of all who are concerned in making our public school system the power for good it is capable of becoming". *Design Technology: Children's Engineering* makes an equally serious claim on the attention of all who are currently struggling to develop a more humane and effective educational system.

Jim Wallace
Graduate School of Professional Studies
Lewis and Clark College

Authors' Note

Design Technology: Children's Engineering is a beginning, an invitation to explore the complexities of teaching and learning. As with any inductive experience, this book will raise issues and questions that launch individual investigations in order to construct personal understanding of design technology. It is also written to present a broad spectrum of ideas that extend thinking about teaching and learning in general.

Underlying the book is the premise that children and teachers need to be actively engaged in the learning process. As designers of their learning, dynamic collaboration between adult and child produces thoughtful curriculum. Thinking required for life-long inquiry becomes embedded in relevant contexts; skills and concepts are developed, in the strongest sense, through the pursuit of one's own questions. Risk taking spurs breakthroughs as adults and children turn frustrated attempts into success. Curiosity and persistence are vital in pursuing future challenges.

This book is not designed to be exclusively a compendium of readily-adapted classroom ideas or engineering techniques. There are other books listed in the end notes that deal in-depth with these topics. Our intent here is to make a contribution to the repertoire of useful strategies for *orchestrating* design technology experiences. The challenge to the reader is to critically examine the ideas presented and creatively design experiences for children.

The chapters of *Design Technology* roughly follow an approximation of the design process, from context to case studies. Illustrations provide the reader with concrete examples that may serve as springboards for further exploration.

Writing this book has been the epitome of a design challenge. We carefully chiseled out our purpose and our intended audience--curriculum innovators, elementary and middle school classroom teachers. We produced elaborate concept webs and demanding timetables, and submitted them to others for their reactions. The plans quickly became amoebic, taking on a life of their own as our progress was impacted by many influences.

It has been an exciting time of practical experience and intellectual challenge. We played with critical questions. *What are the salient features of design technology? How do those features weave together? How can we disentangle them for the reader?* The questions that arose were as energizing as the responses as we created formats and language that we felt best communicated the information.

Throughout the book we refer to the child and teacher using feminine pronouns. "It" was unacceptable, although it implies feminine or masculine gender. Masculine pronouns seem to perpetuate the myths and stereotypes associated with active learning, construction, and tools. We want to highlight the appropriateness of these activities with *all* children and with teachers who have not had previous access to these experiences.

We express our appreciation to the many people who have influenced this book.

To Sybil Coward, Susan's friend who introduced her to the richness of British primary schools over a decade ago. To Peter and Dorothy Twist, and Mary Jefferson who greatly influenced Rob during his British primary teaching experiences in South Yorkshire.

To Andrew Raven who worked with us as we introduced design technology in the Gladstone Schools and later in the Portland, Oregon, area.

To Jim Wallace, Dan Blaufus, Kermit Horn, Angela Loveall, and Jeffry Gottfried for their valuable critiques and suggestions on the manuscript.

To the Gladstone teachers who have embraced the possibilities of design technology and shared their wisdom, imagination, and commitment. Special thanks to Connie Larson, Barbara Eichelberger, Sid Caba, Gail Rupp, Sherie Hildreth, Mary Kilmer, Susan Larfield, Roy DeRousie, Don Michael, and Tom Owen. To the hundreds of additional American and British educators who have shared our journey through our work with The Oregon Museum of Science and Industry and Lewis and Clark College. To Cathy Griswold, Larry Philbrick, and the many others who have trusted the process and taken exciting educational risks in engineering. To Charles Ault for his assistance.

To the children in the Gladstone Schools whose engaging expressions and projects are the subjects of the photographs, whose contemplations encouraged our own wondering and insights, and whose enthusiasm for learning is the heart of the design technology process.

To the many children, educators, and friends who have inspired us through our lives; this book embodies their influence upon our spirit. To Elizabeth Monroe Drews and Robert Sund, Susan's mentors, who helped her shape her own philosophy through their example of commitment and belief. To Debby Kernan, whose support and friendship encouraged Rob to reach for new horizons. Flashes of inspiration, lively conversation, and quiet reflection has helped us create the vision in this book. Of course, any shortcomings in the manuscript are ours alone.

And finally to our editor, Christine Cox, and our publisher, Malcolm Clarkson, whose support and confidence led us to "have courage and trust our intuition".

Susan Dunn   Portland, Oregon
Rob Larson   1990

SUSAN DUNN is currently Director of Staff Development and Curriculum in the Gladstone School District in Gladstone, Oregon. She earned her doctorate in science education from the University of Northern Colorado, with a graduate degree in elementary education from Portland State University and a fine arts degree from Western Washington University. As a classroom teacher and an elementary principal, Susan has worked with children from 3- to 14-year olds. She has also worked extensively with undergraduates and graduates as an assistant professor of education. Her work with children is based on a background in cognitive development and an interest in the integration of curriculum through thematic teaching and project work. Susan's work with educators reveals a respect for collaborative inquiry, risk-taking, and reflection.

ROB LARSON began his formal teaching career in South Yorkshire, England. In his work with children, ages 5 to 15, he has been a classroom teacher and a founding Director of the National Audubon Society Youth Ecology Program. Rob earned an undergraduate degree in elementary education from Western Michigan University and a master's degree in science education from Oregon State University. Currently, as the Manager of Teacher Education at the Oregon Museum of Science and Industry in Portland, Oregon, Rob's interests include informal science and technology learning and the designing of staff development experiences which emphasize the joy of interactive science and technology education.

Both Susan and Rob are associated with Lewis and Clark College as adjunct faculty in the Graduate School of Professional Studies. They have a commitment to child-centered education and a strong belief that teachers are the designers of that experience. Their years of exciting and diverse work with children and teachers are seen in the spirit of *Design Technology: Children's Engineering*.

Design technology is a natural, intellectually and physically interactive process of design, realization, and reflection. Through the consideration of ideas, aesthetics, implications, and available resources, children become imaginative engineers, exploring alternative solutions to contextualized challenges.

Spirit and Context

As I tried my model on the slope I found that it slid rather than rolling slowly. In my design I had not accounted for the rub of the wheels against the chassis. I added some distance to the rods holding the wheels so that they would not touch the car and this fixed the problem. I also had to fix my drawing so that you could see the new spacers. After it went down the ramp a few times I decided to add weights to see the effect. On the graph here you can see that a little weight made it go faster. But after I added quite a few the car became sluggish. I want to work on this. Then I am going to make a bridge with a special crank to open it. I want to make a transportation system.

(8-year-old discussing design technology)

Young children naturally use a design process to transform commonly found materials into imaginative masterpieces. They might create a slope, extend a raceway, or add a garage with boxes from the pantry. While creating these additions to enhance their play, they move beyond a routine and portray experiences with real cars. Youngsters turn over their chairs, add bits of taped paper, and cover the structure with a blanket to build a spaceship. These props propel drama. A sheet, a fiddlehead fern, and some odd pieces from the closet transform the 4-year-old into a feisty pirate character from a beloved bedtime story.

In each case children have determined the context and discovered a real need. They have realized potential solutions and searched for appropriate materials. As the ideas take shape, adjustments are made to satisfy the children's criteria. Other children or adults are often engaged in problem-solving as the children ask questions, talk through a problem, request assistance, or proudly proclaim achievement.

Children involved in active exploration learn that they can influence their environment. They eagerly seek answers to real problems they pose, building and testing theories, creating, and organizing reality in a way that is meaningful to them. This theory of cognitive constructivism provides a perspective for viewing the child as an engineer of personal understanding.

Direct experience allows the child to observe properties and functions of materials. Opportunities arise for sorting, arranging, and recording and form a basis for questions and responsive ideas. Sharing with others opens avenues for the exchange of perspectives. The child is then challenged to review her own ideas in light of new information.

When a situation presents the child with ambiguity or inconsistency, she must make adjustments in her thinking, moving from a strictly sensory dependence to perceiving and constructing patterns and generalizations that might be applied to other situations. She creates an order in her world. Talking helps the child to sort out that order and its meaning. Listening to her as she works with emerging ideas gives insight into conceptual development. Information gained through sensitive observation of the child's playful work opens opportunities and directions for further investigations.

Belief in the child's natural propensity to learn suggests a responsive educational process. It is one that supports an evolution of learning and is constructed as a *negotiation* between partners: child and teacher. That negotiation is based upon an understanding of how children learn and is carried out in learning experiences which are contextualized and meaning-centered. The child and her experience emerge as the centerpiece for a participatory curriculum.

> *When young children lay out a chequerboard garden, or use clay to model a doubledecker bus complete with driver, passenger, and wheels that move, or make rockets from washing-up liquid bottles, they are learning that they can transform the world in some measure to meet their own requirements.*
>
> *The Design Council,*
> *Design and Primary Education*

A child-centered approach to learning envelops the notion that interest, curiosity, and a sense of adventure and discovery are the seeds that develop into meaningful learning. In the process of investigating and understanding her world, a child considers complex interrelationships of perspective, experience, and meaning. Motivated by the need to know, she embraces and shapes opportunities to satisfy an intense urge to make sense of her surroundings. Each individual experience has immediate purpose and value; more importantly, the accumulation of such experience forms a base for future attitudes and understanding. This natural process of learning, and the resulting change, is not prescribed, but discovered.

The teacher's response then, in this negotiated curriculum, is to pose situations in which the child will ask questions and then engage in experiences likely to encompass answers. She begins to link past experiences with emerging information that move her to a deeper level of understanding, into areas that were at one time conceptually unavailable to her.

The child's need to explore is a concrete reminder of humankind's need throughout history to explore, understand, and survive in our environment. Artifacts and structures remain as displays of technological advances. They are evidence of humankind's ability and urge to create, to fashion a response to a perceived need.

From available stone and bones early humans developed tools to aid their hunt for food. Later clay pots were built and fired for carrying water and grain; and a variety of transportation devices were assembled as humans began to move beyond geologic and social barriers. Throughout history, religious rituals and beliefs spurred the construction of great pyramids, temples, and cathedrals.

> *In a certain sense every experience should do something to prepare a person for later experiences of a deeper and more expansive quality. That is the very meaning of growth, continuity, reconstruction of experience.*
>
> John Dewey,
> *Experience and Education*

The child's experience is a metaphor for society's need and ability to connect past experiences and imagination with current challenges which push boundaries to new levels of understanding. Historically humans advance their technological capabilities beyond those of the preceding era through the need to know and the need to respond to societal and environmental demands and opportunities. Today, ancient monuments capture our imagination as we marvel at the precision and grandeur created by more modest tools in the hands of workers with fervent purpose.

The evolution of modern technology enables responses to more current complex challenges.

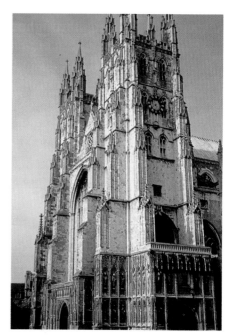

In the recent past, in a generation untouched by the high speed of today's technology, many children came to understand the fundamentals of science and engineering through purposeful application. Children often made their own toys and created household goods that contributed to their learning and lifestyle. In fashioning a corn-husk doll, for example, there may have been a pattern, but the craftsmanship and any modifications belonged to the child. As she carefully observed a model, she would ask many questions. *How were the arms and legs fastened? What tools were used with the materials she selected? What order should the construction take? What were the essential measurements and what could be modified? How would she decorate it?*

Children made dolls, buggies, jumping jacks, boats, and wind-ups. Many were given proudly to others as gifts. Quality came from pride in one's work and was developed through practice with tools, materials, and the process of planning and making. Basic science and math understanding was played out in the realm of toys and pastimes. Notions of aesthetics and craftsmanship were developed through ownership in the process and product.

Today's global community has witnessed a production and information explosion. Technology which has freed us from more mundane tasks has also eliminated many rich contexts for gaining personal understanding of a dramatically changing world. For example, the context of play is often dictated by manufacturers who have marketed highly specific toys, stories, and accessories. At the outset, imagination is directed. Possibilities are limited to those that fall within predefined boundaries. Where repairing items was once a valuable context for technological learning, the sheer quantity and availability of today's mass-produced items lure young buyers to replace rather than to repair the casualties of play.

Modern technology has also intensely distanced adults from understanding the fundamentals of science and technology.

The gap continues to widen between technology and understanding in play and in the workplace. Increased complexity and the inability to keep up with dramatic technological advances have perpetuated dependency on specialization. Items that were once more easily probed and understood now require specialized attention and skills. The rapid accumulation of knowledge has spawned a sense of urgency to master information quickly, perhaps at the expense of building foundational understanding needed for future learning. Quality remains elusive. *More* and *faster* have become mistakenly synonymous with "better ".

In attempts to deal with increasing information, much of today's educational practice has become mechanical. Overburdened curriculum agendas are devoted to rote memory and to filling in blanks, circling responses, and underlining ready-made thoughts in order to *cover* material quickly. Complex tasks that require thoughtful time have been reduced to simple, yet highly abstract, pieces removed from the child's world. Children are seldom asked to observe carefully and pose their own questions.

> *There is no evidence that technical knowledge freely translates into social wisdom. The information age in which we take such pride as a symbol of progress is undermined because that growing base of knowledge does not translate to understanding, especially of what science and technology do to our lives. Thus the paradox of more knowledge and less understanding.*
>
> Edward Wenk,
> *Tradeoffs: Imperatives of Choice in a High-Tech World*

> *Through their actions or, more precisely, interactions with the world, humans construct their own experience and knowledge. Philosophically, this is a constructivist view; it contrasts with mechanistic views, which consider all knowledge to be copied directly from external experience.* George W. Rebok, *Life-span Cognitive Development*

In constantly responding to preconceived ideas, children lose opportunities to demonstrate original thinking, organize concepts, and design formats which capture their intent. *Prescribed* curriculum, an exclusively predetermined learning agenda, ignores the contexts that are naturally created by childhood. Although some elements of prescription have value in planning curriculum, the notion of the "child's curriculum" has long been buried under layers of national, state, district, and school mandates.

Design technology extends natural childhood processes of learning. It allows us to reflect and to inquire about the origins and development of our ideas as it challenges us to critically examine the applicability of our ideas. It provides valuable opportunities for children to tackle practical problems which transcend arbitrary boundaries of specialized subject areas, while inviting rich use of imagination.

Unlike curricular approaches that shy away from complexity, design technology builds on the need to see and address complex interrelationships. It draws its strength from innovative tradition in cognitive psychology and child-centered instruction, and has evolved from a need to view teaching and learning in ways that are meaningful to children. At the same time design technology addresses current challenges in science, technology and engineering education through interdisciplinary strategies.

I built a truck and
it is big. I made it out
of boxes and cardboard.
It is powered with a rubberband. The wheels are round.
I used tape and then I put
wheels on my truck too. Its
wheels are made out of wood.
I tested it and it works. I
wound my truck. It went
five squares with a bag of
sand on it.

The demands of rapidly changing paradigms in science and technology require corresponding paradigm shifts in education. Throughout history the applications of science and technology have evolved as new perceptions modify old beliefs. The discoveries of patterns and relationships bring about new ways to think about science and technology. The metaphor of "building blocks", depicting fundamental parts stacked in a linear progression, is replaced in a complex world by the recognition of interconnections. The webbing of ideas provides many alternative paths for linking concepts and processes, providing for fluidity and flexibility of thought. Responding to increasingly complex challenges suggests that educational efforts become increasingly dynamic.

Engineering with children offers an integrated and balanced approach to inspire innovative thinking and creative perspectives in science and technology. It also provides realistic contexts for language and mathematics. Design technology opens the classroom door to technology and aesthetics. These first-hand experiences afford children and teachers the opportunity to revel in challenge, build confidence, be comfortable with complexity and ambiguity, and delight in the power of their own thinking.

Exploration

There are many entrance and exit points in children's engineering. A child may dive headlong into challenges that emanate from wondering about an enticing material or the application of a technique. She may wander serendipitously into success, momentarily sidetracked from a more laborious plan. And she may abandon schemes prior to completion or add the final touches to a triumphant accomplishment. This may occur in a flash or over an extended period of time.

In setting forth a diagram of the design technology process it quickly becomes apparent that such an attempt results in an oversimplification. The process is a vital, human process, susceptible to variation. Nevertheless, to understand design technology, a starting point is necessary for further investigation. A diagram which captures this complexity becomes a design challenge of its own.

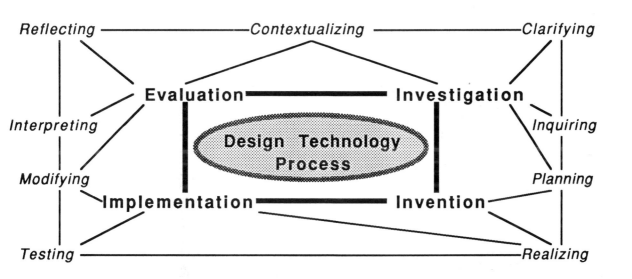

The numerous skills that weave throughout the design technology process generally fall into four major categories: investigation, invention, implementation, and evaluation. The major elements of each category occur recursively, in repeated cycles, as the young engineer progresses through a series of decision points to arrive at a resolution.

Investigation includes the development of context, clarification of the task, and inquiry into an array of options through research. A child in the initial stages of investigation poses a question, becomes aware of a need or problem, or accepts a challenge. She asks focusing questions to locate parameters and gain clarity. The young engineer expands her ideas through design questions, gathers information, and generates many ideas on which to base a tentative selection. At this time the child is beginning to explore the suitability of materials and tools. She works with a variety of resources, notes detail, imposes judgments where discrepancies exist, and begins to develop the major aspects of workable solutions.

The **invention** phase encompasses continued inquiry, planning, and the realization of a design. Alternatives are weighed, eliminated, and combined, based on criteria fitting the child's purpose. The child plans her ideas in graphic and verbal form, detailing particular aspects of the emerging design. Materials, tools, and engineering techniques are chosen and the response to the problem is often fashioned through the construction of a prototype.

The **implementation** of the design poses opportunities to realize, test, and modify the original design. The child examines her creation, experiments with other ideas, and makes modifications in light of her observations. She may also isolate and check variables in designing fair tests and interpreting the reasonableness of the results.

Evaluation of the process and the product is carried out in consideration of predetermined and emerging criteria. The child interprets the results, reflecting on her achievements. She determines the extent to which the design addresses the initial challenge or problem. At some point she may discover a need to make modifications. This review and critique of the process and product often fuel further investigation.

Although the previous diagram shows the relationships between the areas, it might be better represented as a circle. At the time a child completes one cycle and presents a resolution, the process of reflection gives rise to more questions which could potentially sustain the cyclic process through refinement or the evolution of related ideas.

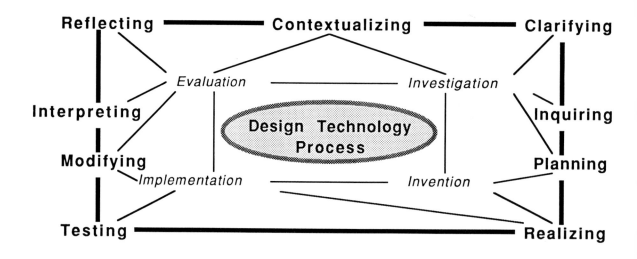

Furthermore, the questions generated at one stage motivate the investigations at the *next* level. The results of each stage are evaluated in terms of the tasks and considerations raised in *prior* stages. Thus, each stage, paired with the preceding stage, forms a loop.

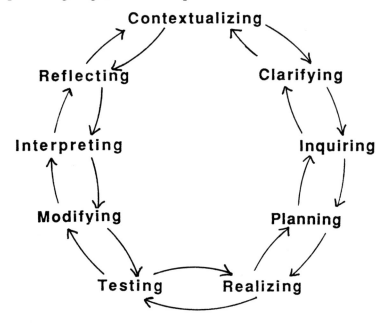

In looking more closely at the larger cycle, the macro-design process, it becomes even more intricate. The decisions at each stage are reflected in, and challenged by, all *subsequent* stages.

Each stage becomes a micro-design cycle as basic questions of investigation, invention, implementation, and evaluation are asked. The model, then, becomes suitably more complex. For example, consider the reflection of a child who has made a humane insect catcher for use in field study. As shown in the diagram on page 23, reflection becomes an integral aspect of each of the remaining areas. These questions might arise in many different conversations, including teacher and child discussions.

Reflection —

— Contextualizing

Why did you select this particular project? How does it relate to what you already know and what you need to know? How did you decide to proceed?

— Clarifying

What questions helped you narrow your task? What criteria did you choose to guide your project?

— Inquiring

What questions expanded your original ideas? What resources did you use? What information was most helpful? How did you record and organize your data?

— Planning

How many plans did you consider? What did they have in common? What features were unique? Why did you select this particular design for development? What form did your plan take? How did it help you?

— Realizing

What materials did you use? What steps did you take in the construction? What problems did you encounter and how did you overcome them?

— Testing

What questions did you ask? What predictions did you make? How did you decide on your method of checking your ideas?

— Modifying

What changes did you make and how did you decide to make them? How did the changes affect your project?

— Interpreting

How did your tests fit your criteria? How did you determine that your observations were reasonable and acceptable? How did you select this format to communicate your results?

Just as reflection is seen throughout the cycle, all stages are integrally related.

In the process of reflection, the child is encouraged to review each stage of the process, to detail her thinking and decisions, and to make judgments about the appropriateness and effectiveness of those decisions. The child may feel the need to return freely to a previous stage for further work or to change directions.

Just as reflection is seen throughout the design technology cycle, *all* stages are integrally related, and in reality, cannot be separated. This constitutes a holographic view of the design technology experience in that each part of the process, or stage, reflects the larger cycle in a condensed form. Contextualizing sets the tone and conditions for the purpose and process. Clarifying, inquiring, and planning give direction to other stages. Each stage calls for interpreting, modifying and testing; realizing a plan becomes a goal for further investigation. With that goal in mind, fluidity in thinking and action helps the child remain spontaneous and flexible, open to changing ideas.

While children explore available options and gain responsibility for their learning in design technology, individual learning strategies become increasingly apparent. The process orientation of design technology is one that embraces the strengths and needs of all learners.

[Design technology processes] can be applied to simple tasks set for the five-year-old in exactly the same way as it is used by much older children wrestling with what would appear to be more complicated problems. The tasks could be exactly the same, the level of sophistication would be determined by age, experience and the individual child's stage of development. Pat Williams and David Jinks, Design and Technology: 5-12

Design technology emphasizes the link among scientific and mathematical principles, language, and elements of planning and display. The experience provides a context for learning a variety of skills and concepts. Process skills are those activities used to gather, shape, evaluate, communicate, and apply information. Arising from the need to know, these skills are taught, practiced or refined in a natural context. Concepts are organizers for related ideas. Children develop and test concepts over time while engaged in first-hand experiences. The combinations of process skills and concepts are determined by the challenge at hand and the direction taken to provide a resolution.

In the investigation stage, concepts evolve from the child's interests and needs in the context of the classroom environment or topic for exploration. In subtle ways the teacher may encourage closer examination of a concept through the orchestration of experiences which generate interest in a given concept. In addition, as a child comes into contact with science concepts, related ideas become known through gentle guidance. This is in contrast to the reliance on deductive techniques which are often used to present a predetermined roster of vocabulary and activities.

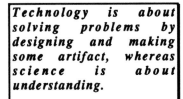

Technology is about solving problems by designing and making some artifact, whereas science is about understanding.

Wynne Harlen,
Teaching and Learning Primary Science

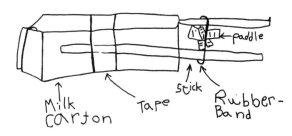

For example, children studying the topic "water" may investigate a rubberband-powered paddleboat. As children set to work they will identify the materials needed, use measurement skills, wrestle with questions of waterproof adhesives and fasteners, and select the most effective size and strength of the rubberbands. These steps require prediction, testing, and modification. Children engage in sharing ideas, graphing race results, drawing diagrams, and writing about their experience. In their explorations they will encounter science concepts of buoyancy, energy, motion, and friction, and grapple with engineering concepts of strength, weight, connecting materials, and durability.

The discovery of attributes of friction may give rise to intuitive understandings of momentum, inertia, and mass. These concepts are investigated in the context of the child's need to understand them, rather than in isolated and often abstract circumstances. In the construction of a vehicle that will move swiftly down a ramp, a child will gain an appreciation of friction as it relates to a companion concept, cause and effect. The child may observe that the wheel rubs against the chassis and creates an opposing force, slowing the vehicle. A response may be to control the friction by inserting a spacer between the wheel and chassis or by investigating axle placement. The child is also working with a host of other related concepts in this example. The value of prediction becomes recognizable in thinking ahead about the most suitable response to the problem. Concepts of velocity (speed and direction) and time are applied in interpreting the results of the modification.

In children's engineering, then, understanding science comes from investigating related technology. Rather than requiring a complete scientific understanding prior to applying it to a product, the child learns those same concepts in investigating their application. Well-placed questions, *What is happening?*, or *How does this work?* may assist the child in extracting those foundational science principles from the technology itself.

The following framework is intended as a guide to facilitate science and technology instruction, and not intended to be used as a prescription. The child's motivation and curiosity will help form the direction of the learning while the teacher's role is to reflect, ask guiding questions, and bring to the surface the concepts and processes the child is discovering. The teacher interprets the needs of the child in relationship to other curricular demands and mediates the discrepancies that exist. The development of such an organizational structure rests on the teacher's understanding and ability to negotiate. Teachers who are able to verbalize the engineering experience at this level are demonstrating the internalization and application of concepts and processes that underscore successful teaching and learning.

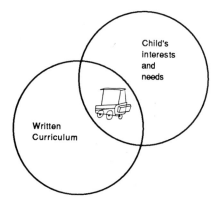

The teacher's ability to see the relationship between the child's interests and needs and the written curriculum is critical for designing meaningful experiences.

A FRAMEWORK FOR THE ANALYSIS OF DESIGN TECHNOLOGY COMPONENTS

DESIGN-TECHNOLOGY

THEME	SCIENCE CONCEPTS	DESIGN CHALLENGES	TECHNICAL APPLICATIONS	PROCESS SKILLS
Transportation	*cause -effect	*Design a rocket which will travel across the room on a line.	*use of shape	*questioning
	*energy		*consideration of durability and strength	*sketching
	*force	*Design a vehicle which will carry a load and deposit it 10 meters away.		*hypothesizing
	*model		*connecting like and unlike materials	*constructing a model
	*scale			*testing
	*system	*Design a transport-ation device which will move something vertically.	*construction of axles	*measuring
	*machine		*placement of fulcrum	*drawing
	*friction		*development of hinges	*labeling
		*Design a self-propelled boat with a steering system	*controlling of friction	*modifying
			*storing energy--use of rubberband power	*negotiating
				*identifying main ideas in the problem
			*application of pneumatic devices--use of tubing, syringes, and balloons	*evaluating
			*consideration for aesthetic qualities	*writing a sequence

The strength of this framework comes from the natural connection that can be shown between curriculum areas, the design challenge, and the inclusion of technical knowledge and processes skills. This example highlights science concepts in particular; however, the format can be changed or extended to include other curriculum areas.

Skills required for mathematical reasoning are also fundamental to the design and construction process. Estimating, computing, and using formulas are examples of skills that can be meaningfully incorporated in the planning and testing of a design. Skills in measurement range from direct application of measuring devices to the use of intermediate systems, scales, ratios, and geometric techniques. A young child may use units such as her foot length or cubes and transfer the information directly to a plan. An older child may use standard units and transfer them to corresponding units on graph paper. Trundle wheels may be used to directly ascertain circumference where more conceptually advanced work may require a compass and protractor. In large-scale work estimation serves as a reasonable beginning, until precision is required. At that point geometric formulas such as triangulation may be applied. Reading and creating tables, graphs, and charts are essential skills in research and presentation. Again, direct representation characterizes the young child's work, whereas an older child may incorporate abstract symbols, multiple variable matrices, exact measurements, and more descriptive language.

> *For most children, practical work provides the most effective means by which understanding of mathematics can develop. It enables them to think out the mathematical ideas which are contained within the various activities they undertake at the same time as they are carrying out these activities.*
>
> *Department of Education and Science, Mathematics Counts (The Cockcroft Report)*

Selecting and combining skills, and applying them purposefully, are primary aspects of mathematical reasoning. Using charts and graphs, the child pulls together chunks of information to develop appropriate mathematical generalizations. Involved with manipulative work, she encounters opportunities for prediction with real-life application. Drawing together mathematical information presented in her plans, she tests the reasonableness of her predictions through construction. Assumptions are tested out in a concrete manner.

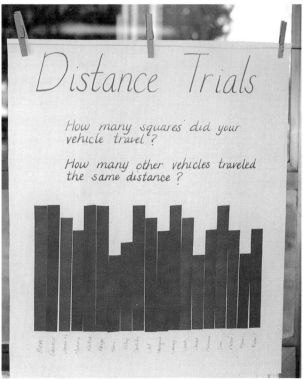

Distance Trials

How many squares did your vehicle travel?

How many other vehicles traveled the same distance?

Natural language development in an educational context springs from the same philosophic foundation as design technology. Each is developed on several premises: learning is greater than the accumulation of isolated sub-skills; the smallest factors in isolation are highly abstract; learning is an interactive process of trial and refinement; and meaning and purpose are central to learning. Out of a need to communicate through reading, writing, speaking, and listening, children synthesize a diverse collection of language skills as tools in developing understanding. Together, skills supply vital clues to augment comprehension of language. As a parallel in engineering, techniques and skills are simply tools used to transform intention to a physical form.

In both cases, any one tool in isolation falls short of creating a complete resolution. Language and engineering skills are more effectively developed and applied in a concrete and purposeful context. Design technology, with its roots in concrete activity, provides a contextual springboard for language development and use. And interaction with language and materials are vital to the process of construction.

Defining a problem and planning a response give the child a purpose for using a variety of language skills. Opportunities arise for the child to listen for specific types of information, to question assumptions and evidence, and to look for fallacies. Working with emerging information she employs language strategies to plan, describe, give directions, and communicate results.

Language provides a window into the conceptual understanding of the young learner as she chatters. The child engages in vivid description, grappling with new questions and ideas spurred by the immediate results of her experimentation. Her initial parlay with a concept will not appear in scientific phrases; but attempts at description, explanation, and design application hint at a more intuitive working understanding. The words come from the need to communicate what she is physically able to investigate with her hands. Labels for concepts, applied after understanding has developed, are then used as handy shortcuts full of personal meaning. They are connected to first-hand experience rather than existing as empty hand-me-downs.

Throughout the design technology process the interplay between reading and writing affords a child rich opportunities to shape information and ideas. Real-life information sources, including books, magazines, directories, labels, game rules, directions, encyclopedias, posters, and letters provide ways in which diverse information is gathered, organized, and presented. Experiences with that variety allow a child to evaluate and select formats which enhance her *own* messages. The child is helped to see how meaning is supported by form and how form contributes to the power of information.

> *The labels for mucilage, whipped library paste, rubber cement, or a glue stick, and solubility of these adhesives, offer larger and more diverse vocabulary possibilities.*
>
> *Catherine Loughlin and*
> *Joseph Suina,*
> *The Learning Environment*

The child compares and contrasts the contents of different references. She combines bits of information to develop generalizations and tests her predictions through further investigation. Her ability to glean main ideas is demonstrated through paraphrasing passages and summarizing longer selections. She develops a pace for reading to fit her purpose and she learns strategies for locating information quickly and organizing her thoughts.

Encouraged to record experiences, the child logs modifications, notes questions, and finds a purpose for a variety of writing. The writing is related to something meaningful in her experience. In sharing the record of her progress in a dialogue journal format, the child invites the teacher to evaluate conceptual development, respond to and pose questions, and provide clarification. The teacher may also use this format to encourage the young designer through written feedback.

I made an angel. Her wings moved up and down. I thought it would be hard to make an ornament with moving parts. I found it was fun. I thought I made the impossible! At the beginning we drew a diagram of how it would work and asked questions like How will I attach the top? What will I make? How will I design it? I learned if you stick to it you can make anything.

All your careful planning and belief in yourself helped you succeed in this project.

I really did somthing that I thought I could not do at first and I did it and I am proud of myself I think that I can do anything I can put my mind to. I can do it! I learned a lot yesterday!

You worked very hard on this project and have every reason to be proud of yourself. Keep up the good work.

When I first saw what we had to do I thought I would never be able to make one. But once I planned it out and started I realized it wasn't so hard. Now I know I should believe in myself more often. I learned not to give up so soon.

Many things in both school and life are easier than they look at first.

When I first started I thought that I would never be able to make one, but I did. I learned so much, but what I really learned was self control and that I don't always need grownups to help with everything. Also I want to thank whoever made up "Rough Drafts" (The word is good enough to frame.)

I agree, rough drafts are a great idea.

Arranging and writing sequential steps provide a review of thinking as well as directions for others to follow. Words are carefully selected to convey a specific message as the child communicates the results of her efforts. Writing for presentation provides a real reason for the child to attend to language conventions in the editing phase. Earlier phases in the writing process focus attention on meaning and the development of supportive formats for intended audiences.

Graphic representations, in the forms of drawings, graphs, and charts, are used to convey the design technology process and its results. The child grapples with the difficulty of transferring an idea to a two-dimensional format. Sketching freezes elusive ideas and provides a format for mental rehearsal as the child mulls over possibilities.

> *Design is that area of inventive, artistic activity concerned with prescribing form, structure or pattern for a proposed man-made artifact or work of art, and depends upon acquired knowledge, analytical and practical skills and decision-making.*
>
> *John Lancaster, Ed.*
> *Art, Craft and Design in the Primary School*

In representing her project in a two-dimensional format, the child selects the medium and technique that best represent its texture and material. She may experiment with different types of paper, color, brushes, or printing implements. She may explore a variety of styles--realistic, impressionistic, or abstract. Point of view may be represented in a number of ways, through orthographic, isometric, oblique, and one-point or two-point perspective renderings.

Transforming a two-dimensional plan to a three-dimensional model is conceptually challenging. The use of grids and dimension in planning graphic displays helps develop an awareness of mathematic relationships and an appreciation of spatial arrangement. Just as a designer or engineer works with multiple drafts, the child needs contemplative time and assurance that refinement is a crucial part of creative endeavors. The project will evolve, possibly through *several* drafts; a final two-dimensional rendering will capture the resulting changes in the original design.

TALKING DOGS

Sketching freezes elusive ideas and provides a format for mental rehearsal as the child mulls over possibilities.

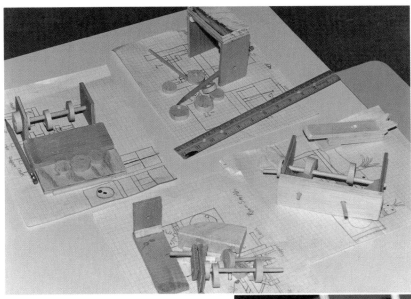

Transforming a two-dimensional plan to a three-dimensional model is conceptually challenging.

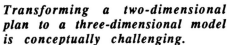

Final touches added to the model present new challenges for imaginative solutions. Detail work requires keen observation and technical skill. The child attends to the shape, pattern, color, contrast, and texture that adorn the three dimensional form. Preparing for presentation, the child uses her calligraphic skills. Labels, captions, information about the construction process, and evaluation are added, artistically arranged to add graphic interest. The completed project is then proudly displayed for viewing.

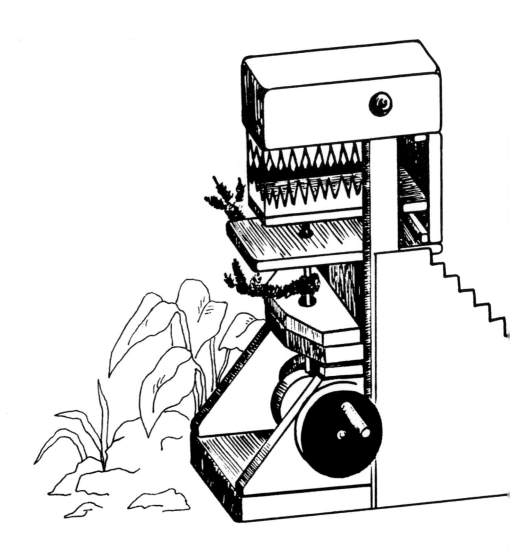

Engineering

Engineering techniques are central to design technology. Basic structural designs, connectors, and applications for materials and systems may be discovered through a child's ingenuity. Experimentation with early drafts or prototypes allows the child to evaluate the strengths and weaknesses of different techniques. Where a more exacting design or a new idea is required, the teacher may elect to introduce a particular strategy or array of options. A sensitively-timed suggestion, in the form of a question or demonstration, may nudge a child past a construction problem. Observations of nature and the human-made artifacts provide clues for structural application. The child's discoveries, in balance with the teacher's guidance, blend in matching technique to purpose. Skillful craftsmanship, the careful execution of technique, ensures a smoother mechanical functioning and a more aesthetically pleasing appearance.

Presented in the following pages are illustrations of and reflection on successful techniques set forth in the context of children's work.

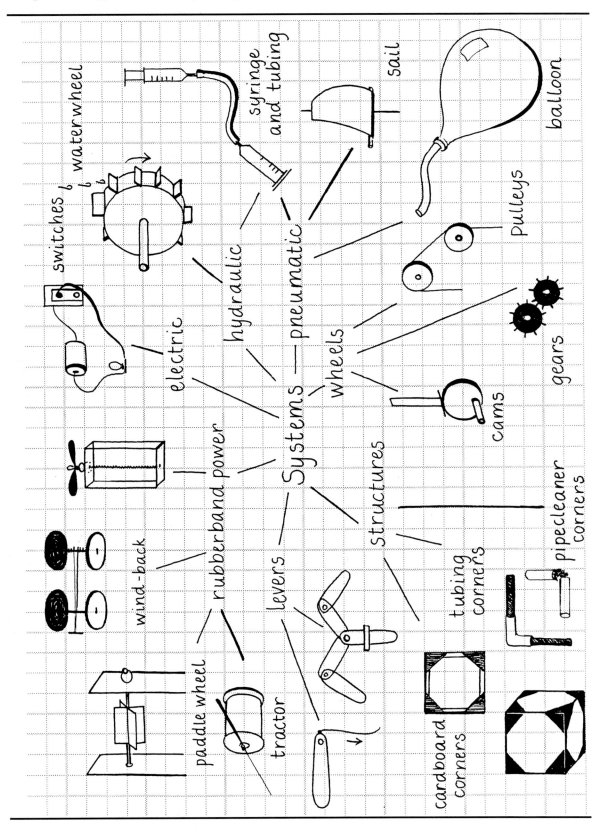

waterwheel

switches

syringe
and tubing

sail

balloon

hydraulic

Systems — pneumatic

Pulleys

electric

wheels

gears

cams

Structures

rubberband power

wind-back

levers

tubing
corners

pipecleaner
corners

paddle wheel

tractor

cardboard
corners

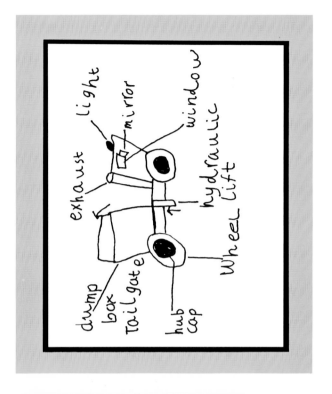

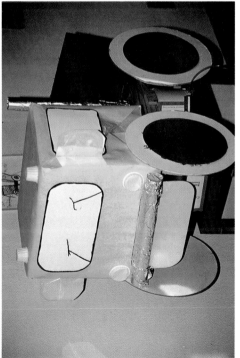

We helped with the
hydraulic pressure.
It tips the dump truck.
I helped put the cubes
in the back of the dump truck.
We were trying to see if it
worked.

Selecting materials for a design is a fitting opportunity to engage children in discussion about their choices and conservation of resources. Materials are selected for their characteristics which fit the demands of the design. Strength, density, flexibility, weight, stability, durability, elasticity, conductivity, pliability and balance may be taken into account. Having a wide selection encourages experimentation and provides for more satisfactory application.

Wise selection of materials and forms may solve particular design problems. Using more material than is needed may add unnecessarily to the weight and cost of the design without additional benefit. Generally, more permanent materials are substituted with more modest supplies in early working models.

Using commonly found materials in imaginative ways can cut down on expenses. Parts of discarded mechanisms have countless possibilities and may be used creatively to replace less accessible supplies. Recycling these materials also reduces waste and environmental pollution, and adds to the material treasury.

As children are confronted with a variety of challenges the need arises for an equally diverse repertoire of skills in materials use. Developing techniques for altering, connecting, and combining materials increases the variety from which the children will select. For example, children who are acquainted with the flexibility and adhesive qualities of tape may apply large quantities to act as a hinge for a box lid. They may discover the tape does not blend with their aesthetic intent and after many uses wears thin. Cloth hinges present a more attractive and durable possibility. It is only when the children are able, through experience, to apply the material and its attributes to a functional purpose that they are empowered to create their own designs.

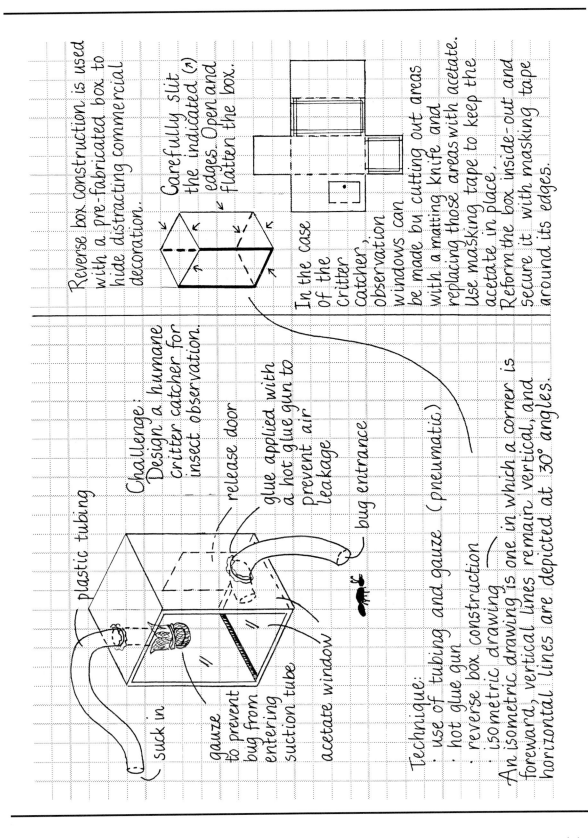

Reverse box construction is used with a pre-fabricated box to hide distracting commercial decoration.

Carefully slit the indicated (↗) edges. Open and flatten the box.

In the case of the critter catcher, observation windows can be made by cutting out areas with a matting knife and replacing those areas with acetate. Use masking tape to keep the acetate in place. Reform the box inside-out and secure it with masking tape around its edges.

plastic tubing

Challenge: Design a humane critter catcher for insect observation.

release door

glue applied with a hot glue gun to prevent air leakage

bug entrance

suck in

gauze to prevent bug from entering suction tube

acetate window

Technique:
· use of tubing and gauze (pneumatic)
· hot glue gun
· reverse box construction
· isometric drawing
An isometric drawing is one in which a corner is forward, vertical lines remain vertical, and horizontal lines are depicted at 30° angles.

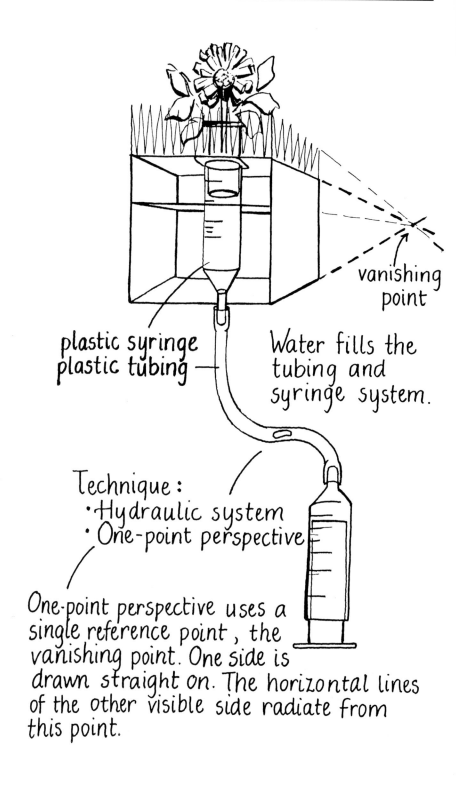

vanishing
point

plastic syringe
plastic tubing —

Water fills the
tubing and
syringe system.

Technique:
• Hydraulic system
• One-point perspective

One-point perspective uses a
single reference point, the
vanishing point. One side is
drawn straight on. The horizontal lines
of the other visible side radiate from
this point.

Materials science is recognized as a relatively new scientific field which draws upon the chemical and physical properties of materials. It is the investigation of material attributes and transformations to fit intended uses in design. A range of possibilities for materials use can be described by using the three-dimensional model shown below. In conceptualizing a design, young engineers take into account a variety of variables - available *materials*, applied *engineering concepts*, and *engineering processes*. These are needed to transform material to suit a design purpose. Children can be involved in creating such a model to generate a range of techniques to use with available material. Variables may change depending on the context of the activity and the skills of the children.

Materials Science Model

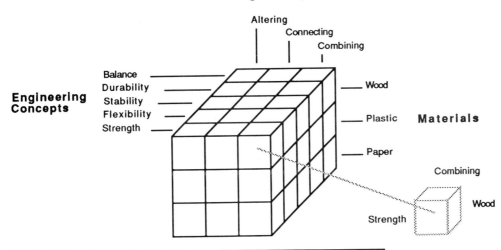

In order to make wood stronger, soaked paper reduced to mush might be combined with water-soluble glue resulting in a strengthened dried material. One might connect layers of wood with glue, alternating grain directions in a laminating process. Connecting rolled tubes with wood glue provides structural strength. Wood might also be made more flexible by altering it, using soaked thin pieces that can be easily bent. Paper can be made stronger by rolling, folding, and ribboning as in corrugation. Adding a veneer to cardboard or wood increases durability with a plastic coating.

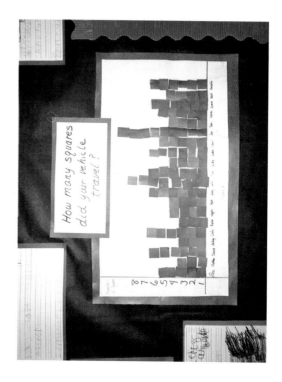

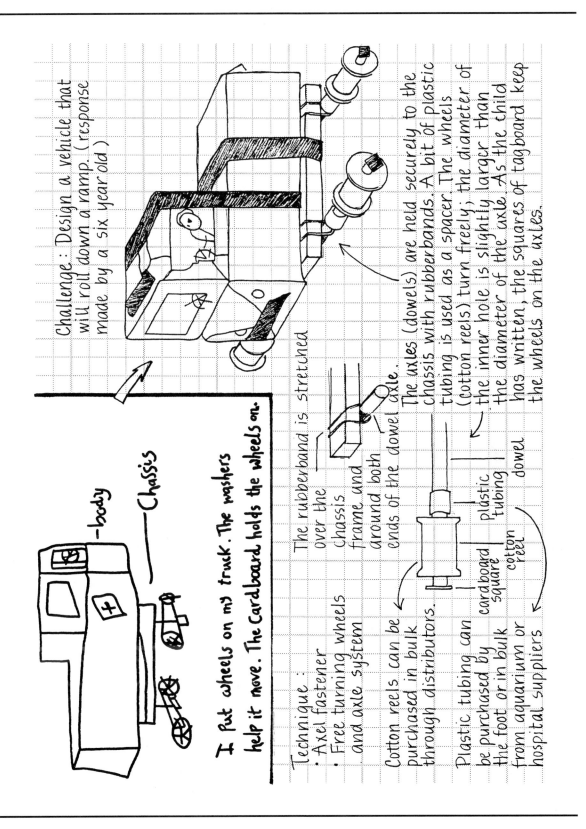

Challenge: Design a vehicle that will roll down a ramp. (response made by a six year old.)

—body

——Chassis

I put wheels on my truck. The washers help it move. The cardboard holds the wheels on.

Technique:
- Axel fastener
- Free turning wheels and axle system

Cotton reels can be purchased in bulk through distributors.

Plastic tubing can be purchased by the foot or in bulk from aquarium or hospital suppliers.

The rubberband is stretched over the chassis frame and around both ends of the dowel axle.

cardboard square | plastic tubing
cotton reel | dowel

The axles (dowels) are held securely to the chassis with rubberbands. A bit of plastic tubing is used as a spacer. The wheels (cotton reels) turn freely; the diameter of the inner hole is slightly larger than the diameter of the axle. As the child has written, the squares of tagboard keep the wheels on the axles.

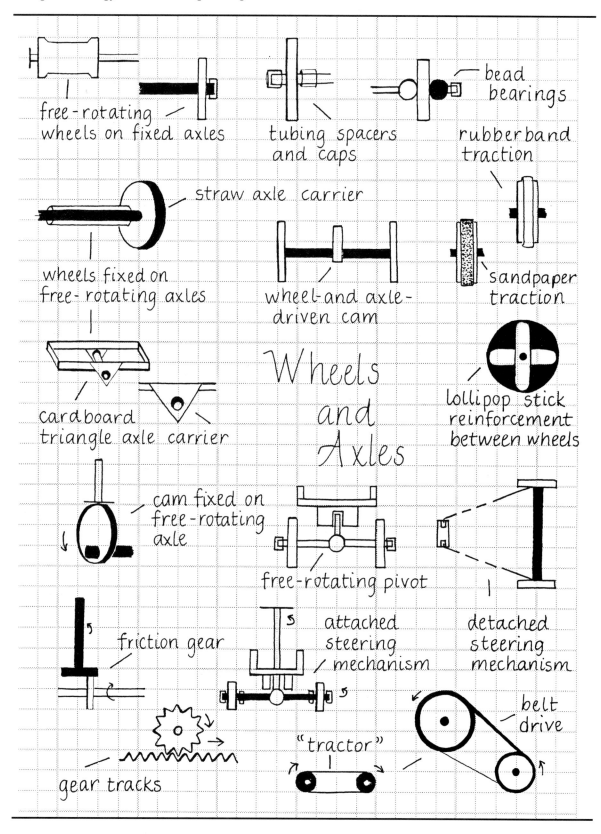

free-rotating
wheels on fixed axles

tubing spacers
and caps

bead
bearings

rubber band
traction

straw axle carrier

wheels fixed on
free-rotating axles

wheel-and axle-
driven cam

sandpaper
traction

cardboard
triangle axle carrier

Wheels
and
Axles

lollipop stick
reinforcement
between wheels

cam fixed on
free-rotating
axle

free-rotating pivot

attached
steering
mechanism

detached
steering
mechanism

friction gear

belt
drive

gear tracks

"tractor"

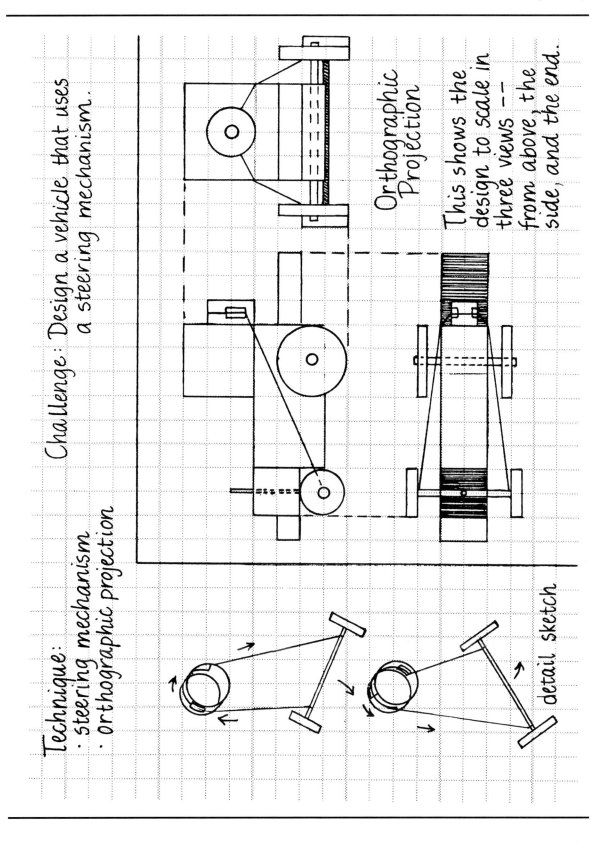

Challenge: Design a vehicle that uses
a steering mechanism.

Technique:
· steering mechanism
· orthographic projection

Orthographic
Projection

This shows the
design to scale in
three views —
from above, the
side, and the end.

detail sketch.

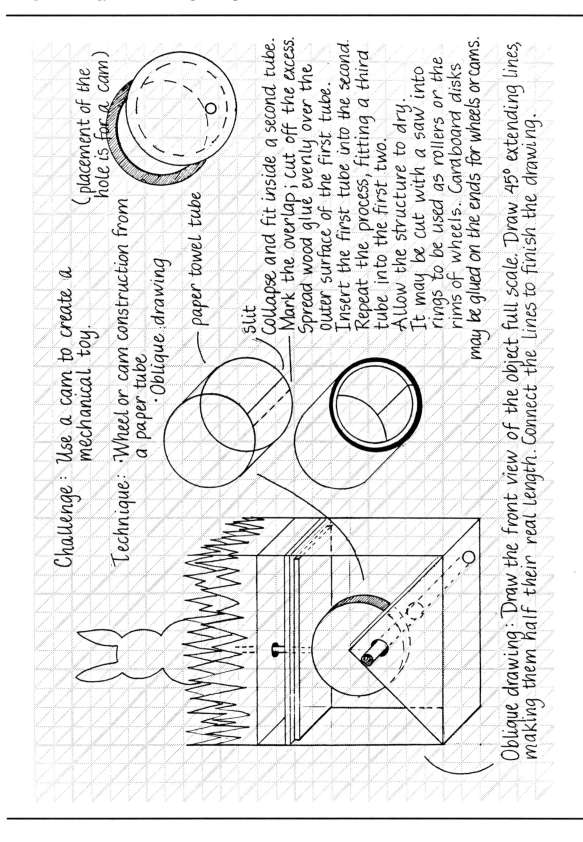

Challenge: Use a cam to create a mechanical toy.

Technique: Wheel or cam construction from a paper tube.
·Oblique drawing

(placement of the hole is for a cam)

paper towel tube

slit

Collapse and fit inside a second tube. Mark the overlap; cut off the excess. Spread wood glue evenly over the outer surface of the first tube. Insert the first tube into the second. Repeat the process, fitting a third tube into the first two. Allow the structure to dry. It may be cut with a saw into rings to be used as rollers or the rims of wheels. Cardboard disks may be glued on the ends for wheels or cams.

Oblique drawing: Draw the front view of the object full scale. Draw 45° extending lines, making them half their real length. Connect the lines to finish the drawing.

Stability of structures can be enhanced through techniques of bracing. For example, middle school children attempting to build tall structures, with limited time and materials, found that some sort of bracing was necessary to support the mass of their structure. After overnight preparation, some teams returned to their "construction site" with rolled newspaper and attempted to create a long tube. When it was vertically erected, the tower collapsed. Children then scurried to add diagonal props. Other teams came prepared dragging prefabricated newspaper rectangles with cross-supports. The diagonal inserts that connected corners, a triangulation technique, added rigidity to their structure.

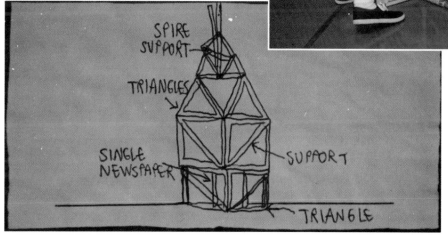

Triangulation, arches, and columns have been used in designs that span centuries.

A basic structure for engineering may be applied to assist children in connecting materials. The technique, a "cardboard corner", utilizes triangular pieces of card to connect pieces of wood. A rectangle is formed using four pieces of wood. Each joint is glued and secured with a triangle that overlaps the adjacent sides. A total of eight triangles, one at each of the four corners, repeated on the opposite side of the structure, provides a sturdy rectangle. Children may adapt this technique to the construction of models that require a variety of shapes and angles.

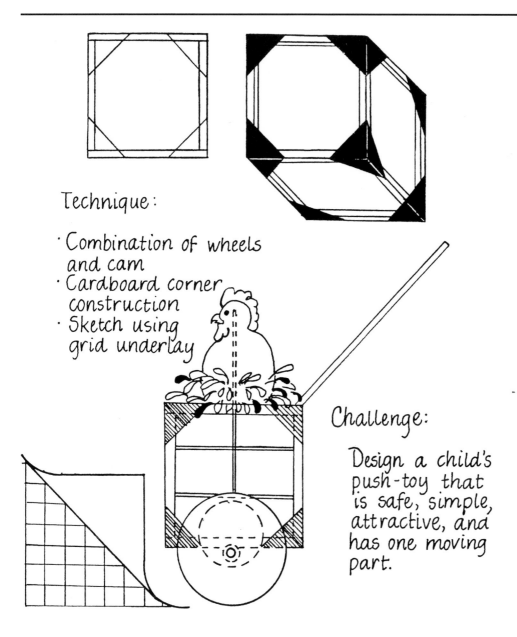

Technique:

· Combination of wheels and cam
· Cardboard corner construction
· Sketch using grid underlay

Challenge:

Design a child's push-toy that is safe, simple, attractive, and has one moving part.

Materials can also be connected through the inventive use of other common supplies. Pieces of tubing can be cut and used to join lengths of dowel. The flexibility of tubing makes it a suitable joint for corners. Pipe cleaners may be inserted into straws to create the same effect. The advantage of this method is in the ability to bend the pipe cleaner and retain a shape.

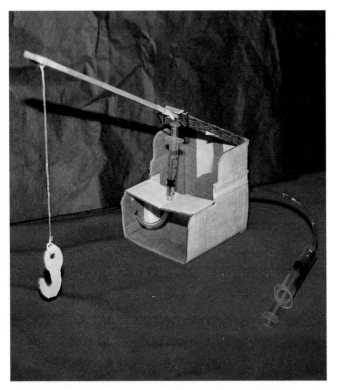

Children record initial ideas in sketches. Just as with the writing process, they use early drafts to focus on ideas without being overly concerned about conventions and precision. As they work through plans, constructing, testing, and modifying their original designs, children may employ drawing to record those changes.

As children become more sophisticated in their thinking and skillful in their drawing, they will increase their repertoire to include more complex forms of graphic representation. Children will need practice in order to become adept at using perspective, isometric, oblique, and orthographic projections. These require consideration of more than one surface at a time.

Planning with younger children often necessitates adaptations. Teachers may find it beneficial to have on hand a supply of cut paper shapes for the children to arrange and paste. The manipulation of concrete elements, before deciding on a final plan, allows them to try several possibilities without the tedious frustration of erasures.

Helpful tools for young draftsmen include well-sharpened pencils, clean erasers, colored pencils, ink pens, lined and graph paper, tracing and drawing paper, rulers, and templates. Children can learn to use graphic hints to record textures, lighting conditions, and details. These require time and concentration, and are often reserved for the later stages of presentation. Final presentation graphics are attractive and accurate, often supporting the main idea through the use of color, composition, and careful lettering.

The engineering of a creative design, whether in thought or three-dimensional rendering, suggests a variety of skills. Choosing appropriate tools and materials, applying artful technique in a new context, and developing a product of sound form and viable function can challenge children to new levels of understanding. These challenges are often most effectively addressed in working with other people.

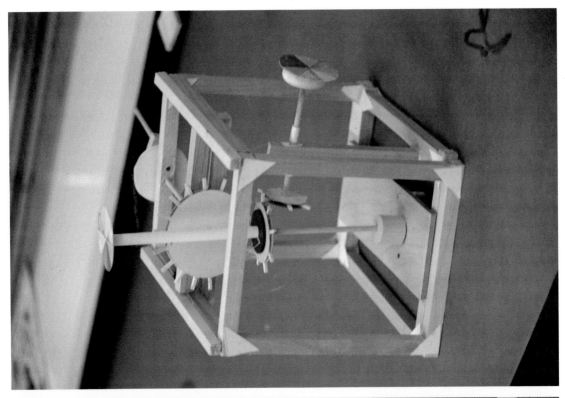

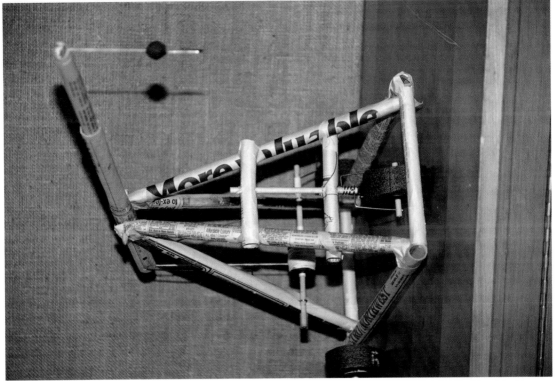

The sharing of ideas and thoughts, through oral rehearsal, not only helps the child to understand her own reasoning, but provides insight into conflicting and complementary perspectives.

Collaboration

Rick: I turned the crank and the cam
pushed the dowel up, but it won't
slide back.

Jayne: Let me take a look.

Rick: I think the dowel's too big to slide
back down

Jayne: Well, you could sand down the
dowel...or make a bigger hole with
the rasp.

Rick: Okay, I'll use the rasp.

Jayne: I'd try candle wax on the dowel. It
might make it slide easier, too.

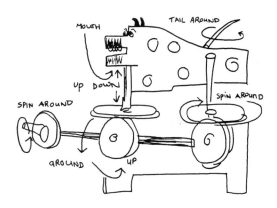

Working with one another provides opportunities for collaboration in contemporary educational experience. Cooperative inquiry, an approach to problem finding and solving, has been shown in countless ways to be a sound and practical educational strategy. In design technology, children and teachers work together through negotiation to achieve mutual goals as they adopt multiple roles of questioner, helper, and reflector. The language developments discussed in "Exploration" spring from the need to describe, explain, and share quiet contemplation or the excitement of discovery. And children feel empowered as inquiry leads to discovery and others join in celebration of their increasing ability to make sense of a complicated world.

Central to the collaborative process is the exchange of perspectives and insights. The sharing of ideas and thoughts, through oral rehearsal, not only helps the child to understand her own reasoning, but provides insight into conflicting and complementary perspectives. The child will naturally engage a neighbor or project partner in dialogue replete with incremental understandings and questions which guide further inquiry. Often a subtle suggestion or well-placed question can release the excitement of a new idea or a new-found view.

The open teacher, like a good therapist, establishes rapport and resonance, sensing unspoken needs, conflicts, hopes, and fears. Respecting the learner's autonomy, the teacher spends more time helping to articulate the urgent <u>questions</u> than demanding right answers.
                                    Marilyn Ferguson, The Aquarian Conspiracy

The child's language provides a collage of rich educational texture. The use of language during the design technology process may involve a fantasy or a critical reflection on a given topic, providing a window into the child's sense of meaning. As she talks about her actions and ideas with an active listener, the exchange of viewpoints alters or confirms the child's thinking about her purpose or plan. This dialogical process assists the learner in articulating her strategies and her conceptual understanding. It also makes available, for the astute teacher, an array of information useful for interpreting conceptual difficulties and successes.

The teacher-child relationship offers ample opportunity to reflect and project experience through the use of divergent questions. Divergent questions promote diversity. They allow for a number of responses which are relevant to the child's purpose. They encourage young designers to expand their ideas. Children are invited through these open-ended questions to extend imagination and put together information in new forms. They are asked to make observations, explain their ideas, and project the outcomes.

Consider the building of a printing press for producing a class playbill...*What types of simple machines might be included in your printer? How can we produce a reverse image? How can you control the pressure of the printer? What will happen if you tighten the rubberband joining the two tins?*...Gentle guidance through questioning allows children to explore, expand, and redirect their own questions; sensitive listening encourages reflection, feelings of trust, and a blush of pride. As a result, a partnership is formed between the teacher and child as they work together in pursuit of resolutions.

Where it is obvious that a child has hit a conceptual roadblock the teacher may offer a guiding question that inherently suggests a reasonable possibility. The suggestion may be in the form of an encouraging word or the introduction of different material. Also, in helping the child reflect, the teacher may choose to engage with the child in musing, rephrasing the child's own question, perhaps emphasizing a particular point with inflection or gestures that hint at possibilities. These possibilities, in line with the child's purpose, ability and immediate intention, support independent thinking and respect the child's decision-making. The clues that encourage the advancement of ideas must be kept in perspective as the teacher works with the information the child presents and accepts the decisions the child makes. Through this social exchange, children are able to consider perspectives, appreciate patterns, envision resolutions, foresee consequences, and evaluate ideas and processes.

Children also form cooperative partnerships with each other. In working together they grapple with the identification and clarification of a problem, sort out definitions, and introduce their own questions. At times there may be rough spots as the relationships form and the teacher may enter as another partner to assist the children in the negotiation of their roles.

The clarification of roles is a key element in the success of any cooperative venture. Through guided classroom interaction children work toward a realization that roles differ, overlap and change with time. A skillful teacher helps children identify the roles that emerge from the children's purpose and plan. Through discussion the value of different roles are appreciated and children match their abilities and interests to their initial responsibilities.

For example, children working on group-designed pop-up books initially divided their roles along the lines of recorder, resourcer, and process observer. Later, the same children divided the tasks they defined according

to their interests and expertise. All of the children gathered information for their writing while the pop-up technology, binding, graphics, and calligraphy tasks were picked up by individuals. Although some specialization occurred, all of the children in the group had ownership in the final product. In fact, the children stepped in to assist each other during periods of intense activity with a particular task or when an extra pair of hands was needed.

> *Children with special talents can come into their own in project work. Not only can they contribute their speciality to their group work, but they may also act as 'consultant' to the rest of the class for particular tasks...Children with special talents do not have to spend all their time using them, at the expense of doing other things. This would prevent them from developing other equally important abilities and would deprive other children of the opportunity to practise and learn skills which come easily to these certain children...'Consultant' children help others and themselves at the same time.*
>
> *David Wray, Project Teaching*

As the project progresses they may find that their roles naturally overlap, and in some cases appear to conflict. This is an important aspect of collaborative learning. Reflecting the larger society, classroom project responsibilities are acknowledged as fluid, flexible and adaptable. Through negotiation children come to understand that their initial role may change over time as new issues arise and potential contributions are realized.

Discussing an experience at its conclusion will help the child learn about the importance of *each* role and its interdependence. Articulating the responsibilities of another will help the child sharpen her appreciation of that role's function. In later experiences, children will be more able to change roles and extend their own competence.

In many cases, the translation of a challenge may alter its meaning and children will need to arrive at a common understanding of the task in order to pursue their responses. Each child brings to a cooperative endeavor her own interpretation of the task at hand. *What are we going to do? How much time do we have? What resources do we have?* Through discussion, ideas are synthesized and critiqued in a process to develop a common meaning. This involves questioning and negotiation, a give and take between partners working together toward a mutual goal.

With a goal in mind the children generate ideas to address their challenge. Through encouragement and practice they develop a diversity of options. When children consider the *range* of possibilities the list is more likely to include a number of effective resolutions. As work progresses and initial developments fall short of expectations, there is a collection of ideas to which they can return. Conversely, a simplistic view or premature attachment to *one* solution limits the options and possibly the effectiveness of a satisfying resolution.

As a project evolves children develop camaraderie and share an investment in project success. The need for collective modification of a design becomes increasingly apparent. Children "talk-out" the reasonableness of their ideas and construct notions of variables and fair testing.

Scientists and engineers work mostly in groups and less often as isolated investigators. Similarly, students should gain experience sharing responsibility for learning with each other. In the process of coming to common understandings, students in a group must frequently inform each other about procedures and meanings, argue over findings, and assess how the task is progressing. In the context of team responsibility, feedback and communication become more realistic and of a character very different from the usual individualistic textbook-homework-recitation approach.

AAAS, Science for All Americans

Collaboration may also occur outside the parameters of a group project. Children share materials and ideas that relate to similar work or that have a connection to work of a different nature. In one case, Joel excitedly called across the room to Katie about the discovery he made while making a window frame. He found that positioning a toothpick at an angle, to hold a straw upright while the glue set, allowed him the freedom to turn to more productive tasks. Katie had a similar problem with the house wall. Using Joel's idea, and a dowel to prop up her larger construction, she employed a successful adaptation of a discovered technique.

Just as collaboration provides rich opportunities for children, the same benefits become available to teachers who work in collaborative partnerships. Collegial study groups extend a forum for sharing and developing mutual support. They allow teachers to move further into unchartered adventures with courage to take new risks in teaching and learning. As teachers talk about their work, they are able to reflect, engage in self-evaluation, consider options and perspectives, and exchange ideas for development of classroom environments, evaluation strategies, resources, and project work. The suggestions offered by colleagues will be tempered by the teacher's understanding of her own classroom and will assist her in shaping innovative practices.

The spirit of the design technology process relies on the development of collaborative inquiry. It is through collaboration among children and adults that children are able to experience a *full* sense of exploration and celebration. Artful techniques in creating atmospheres that allow children to engage in collaboration to this degree require investigating what may be called classroom "choreography".

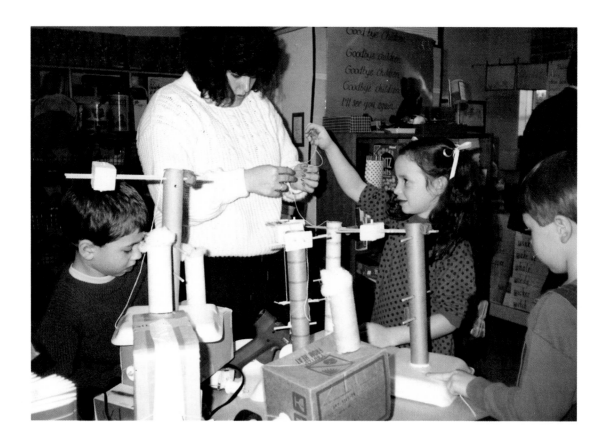

Choreography

In providing design technology experiences for children, attention must be given to a vast array of instructional considerations. Management of design experiences, through planning, negotiation, and an understanding of physical organization reflects a need for teacher intent *and* flexibility. In artfully addressing physical, social, and instructional needs of the child, the teacher orchestrates a composite of instructional variables. This resultant choreography poses for the teacher a design challenge of an instructional sort.

Teachers forecasting an engineering experience will engage in the same planning activities as children undertaking a project. They will consider options and pursue a direction understanding that its course may take on different characteristics as it is influenced by the vitality of the classroom. Children's interests and abilities will tug at the teacher's initial plan, or forecast. A facilitative teacher will use that information to help shape the experience. This planning process is *dynamic* and open to integrating emergent information.

In developing design technology experiences for children teachers employ inductive approaches to concept development. Beginning with experiences central to the child's world the teacher builds opportunities for exploration and expression of developing concepts. New learning emerges from the context of topic-based instruction as children manipulate ideas and materials. Children work with these new ideas, making connections with past experience to better understand the world.

Teachers may find it useful to forecast the development of particular processes and concepts through a framework such as the example on page 27, a concept web, or a subject web. This phase of initial planning is essential for anticipating children's needs for materials, resources, and working conditions of time, space and group patterns.

A concept web radiates from a central theme to subtopics broken into related concepts. These concepts are needed to develop the central theme more fully.

In a subject web, connections are diagrammed to highlight the relationships among curriculum areas and forecasted experiences.

The children may help develop the initial web by offering what they already know about a particular topic. This serves as a starting point for the teacher in assessing the group's background knowledge and allows the children to share previous experiences. Beginning with what children know about a topic, a motivational context is established with a "need to know". From this base a natural progression moves the class into exploring what they want to know.

In further discussion, children are encouraged to pose their questions about the topic for group consideration. The teacher may find it useful to visually display the children's questions through a question web. The children's question web may serve as a natural organizer of sub-topics to be followed up by groups or individuals and later shared with the entire class. It can also point to the need for particular resources or experiences to fill out the development of the topic.

> *...the true teacher knows you can't impose learning. You can, as Galileo said, help the individual discover it within. The open teacher helps the learner discover patterns and connections, fosters openness to strange new possibilities, and is a midwife to ideas. The teacher is a steersman, a catalyst, a facilitator - an agent of learning, but not the first cause.*
>
> *Marilyn Ferguson,*
> *The Aquarian Conspiracy*

A question web is a visual organization of questions that spring from a central theme.

In much the same way, a web may be constructed before moving into design work. The focal point is the design challenge and the children's questions about it radiate from that center. Developing such a web provides thinking time at the outset. It allows the children to anticipate and share their needs and ideas *before* diving headlong into their projects. Throughout the project, the children may continue to add their questions to the web. They may also record their findings in another color to share information and expertise with classmates.

Similar to a question web, the design challenge web allows children to project questions and ideas throughout the design process.

Initial planning charts may prove helpful for young engineers developing a range of possibilities from which to work. They may be encouraged to brainstorm many ideas quickly as a group, recording those ideas for further consideration and development. Individually they may sketch out their initial response to a challenge, its advantages, and areas that need further work. Looking at the original range, children are able to pick out elements of effective designs and recast them in another form. Returning to the earlier example of the printing press, found in *Collaboration,* the range of options may look like this:

MAKING A PRINTER	
IDEAS	WORKING DETAILS
roller pushed with handle	• simple, easy inking, • like a steamroller
roller dragged by a buggy	• a roller • could be motorized
two rollers connected	• like a real printer with the picture on one roller. • How will we ink it ?
flat press	• needs a lot of pressure • like a waffle-maker
printer slider and rotater	• slides to ink pad, rotates, and slides to print • includes inking plan

Early drawings help the group envision an array of possibilities for development.

Inductively, children may also generate rubrics, or open sets of criteria through extracting the *successful* qualities of models. Children use examples of work and talk about the features which are "good". Using the children's language, the teacher lists the ideas that surface through discussion. In developing such a list, a rubric is not artificially imposed; it comes from the children's experiences and perceptions. Children in early drafting and prototyping stages can use the rubric to develop, reflect on, and modify their designs and craftsmanship. The list of criteria will change and grow as the children are exposed to more work samples and become more cognitively sophisticated; it is naturally matched to the children's ability to recognize increasingly complex attributes.

Formative planning takes place, often spontaneously, as the teacher works closely with the children. She will seize the essence of a child's struggle and ask a probing question designed to help the child break through a conceptual problem. In a more lengthy timeframe, the teacher will carefully watch the activity of the class and make changes in the environment to enhance groupwork, movement, and safety. Resources, materials, and tools may be added as a result of keen observations.

Away from the hum of a busy classroom the teacher may reflect on the day's activities and plan modifications to accommodate the children's needs. Observations may yield plans for intervention to assist a group or individual. The teacher may envision planning questions similar to the following: *How can I assist Tonisha with her display work? How can the existing workspace be modified to fit the use of new cutting tools and bulkier materials? How can Jason be involved in the group's work after his absence?* These types of planning occur over a variety of timespans, just as children's planning may be swift or laborious, a short-term trial or a contemplated scheme.

> *There are naturally limits on what children are capable of at various ages, but one thing is certain. If they are never given the chance to try, and sometimes to make a complete mess of the whole process, they will never become capable.*
>
> *David Wray, Project Teaching*

Planning also may occur at the close of an experience as an extension for both teachers and children. This planning responds to questions raised by observations, to further develop inklings that have emerged, and to elaborate on valuable processes and concepts that have emanated from the earlier experience. Children are asked to share their perspectives. *What went well? What challenges did you face? And how did you meet those challenges?* This stage in planning also attempts to establish future working expectations through the critique of the group process.

Children discuss ways in which they successfully worked together. Their strengths as helpful group members are highlighted and celebrated as important contributions to the classroom ethos. Areas where they feel they need more concentration are listed elsewhere. In future working situations positive practices are recounted to affirm the children's abilities. The children and the teacher may select an area from the other list for focus and discussion. In this manner, the children continue to see an accent on positive actions and continue to grow in areas that are deemed important to their learning.

Time is a valuable resource in any classroom. Questions about time are raised in reference to the amount of time devoted to project work each day and the overall time allotted to a project. It is necessary to forecast a targeted ending date and establish a flexible timeline that is responsive to changing classroom circumstances. The teacher may use a classroom project calendar to help children set personal timelines within the framework of the larger timetable. Referring back to previously developed planning webs, the teacher and children may draw elements to include in this schedule.

Learning to break apart larger tasks and sequence intermediate steps moves children toward independence in tackling future tasks that involve complex work over time. Large blocks of time allow children to develop concentration and it may be necessary to adjust and combine previously established routine times to provide those extended time periods. It is important that the teacher declare a plan for how and when the work will take place.

> *The amount and the frequency of time that is allotted to project work varies greatly. Often it reflects the importance given to it...Teachers will, of course, decide for themselves, but bear in mind that children will usually value the things their teacher obviously values, and they are very adept at perceiving which activities are really valued in their classroom.*
> *David Wray, Project Teaching*

Project work may be timetabled as a separate section of the day or it may be integrated into predetermined time slots where there is a match with subject matter. Developing a schedule may become a math lesson, note taking and technical writing skills may be taught or reinforced during a language arts block. Another option is to build management structures into the school day that allow children to move more freely, with teacher assistance, between project work and other requirements. The craft with which a teacher shapes and uses time is dependent upon her ability to see and organize connections between the project and the expressed curriculum schedule.

MONDAY	TUESDAY	WEDNESDAY	THURSDAY	FRIDAY
·Discuss challenge · Groups to explore challenge ·Class question web 5	6	·Put initial ideas on class chart 7	·Discuss effective elements/ combinations 8	·Detail initial plans · Calendars 9
12	← Sketches → 13	← Research/prototype development → 14	15	·Prototype designed 16
·Class sharing ·Rubric 19	← Modifications → 20	21	← Construction / testing → 22	23
←Scale drawings 26	and technical writings → 27	← Reflective template / response → ← Display → 28	29	Final display for parents' visitation 30

Journal entries (vertical label, left side)

Project time during afternoons; also integrated into the appropriate subject time.

Items included on the class project calendar may come from earlier planning webs.

MONDAY	TUESDAY	WEDNESDAY	THURSDAY	FRIDAY
I will draw my idea. 12	I will talk to my partner. 13	I want to try a lot of different materials. 14	I might need to talk to somebody about it. 15	I will finish building my plans. 16
I need to write an invitation to my mom. 19	I might make some changes. 20	I will build my plans — 21	- - - - → 22	23
I need to make a scale drawing. 26	I will write the directions. 27	I will draw an outline. 28	I need to make the display. 29	I will finish my project. 30

Sequencing tasks within a larger context prepares children for independent learning.

Safety, space, and storage become important considerations in investigating the physical organization of successful design technology experiences. Attention to these physical needs provides the teacher with opportunities to maintain fluidity in instruction and movement while offering consistent standards of safety and materials use.

The varied forms of shaping tools offer possibilities for thinking processes. It seems natural to compare the roughness of sandpaper with the sharpness of a carpenter's plane and the evenness of a putty knife, as each tool is used to produce a smooth surface. The smooth point on an awl, the spiraling grooves of a drill bit, and the blunt end of a hole punch are different, inviting children to think about functional reasons for each.

Catherine Loughlin and
Joseph Suina,
The Learning Environment

Tools are chosen which best fit the child's ability and the task. Different materials, and particular results with similar materials, require a careful selection of tools. Ordinary scissors are used to cut paper, whereas sewing shears are more appropriate for cutting fabric. Matting knives with metal rulers may be used for intricate tag board incisions, but a paper cutter would more effectively slice a large sheet of tag with a straight edge. Sawing a wooden dowel with a right-angle end requires a child's saw; a curved cut in wood requires the thin blade in a coping saw. In all cases a match among the tasks, materials and tools will more likely result in a satisfactory outcome and safety for the child.

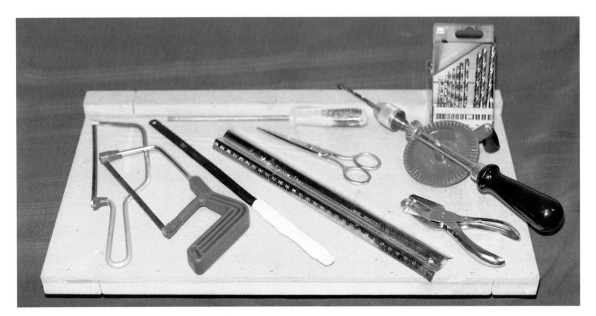

Handling tools requires attention to both psychological and physical safety. A child *must* receive instruction in the proper use, carriage, and storage of tools *prior* to their use. The careful modelling of techniques offers the child confidence and skill; both are needed for successful implementation.

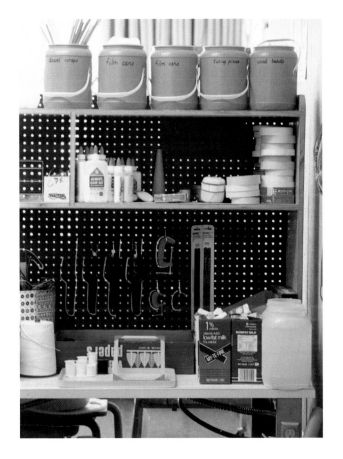

Tools should be operated and carried point down. Locating and using tools at specific worksites eliminates the need to transport them. Storing tools and materials in easily identified containers permits easy access. Inventories, or outlines marking the placement of tools, allows their use and return to be easily monitored. Promptly replacing lost or broken tools avoids a backup of eager workers and resulting impatience. Tools should be kept in good working order; dull tools rip and splinter materials and frustrate the attempts of enthusiastic engineers.

Large workspaces provide elbow room for exuberant large muscle work. Individual desk tops make excellent sites for sawing; resulting table movement affects only one work station. Table tops can be preserved with the use of a cutting board under materials that are being sawed, drilled, or glued. Spaces that accommodate larger construction and group work should be considered in the set-up plan. Classroom pathways should be kept clear for free movement. Close detail work requires an area where there is little distraction or traffic as steady hands and concentration are necessary for intricate elaboration.

Storage space for project work in progress requires imagination and modifications in most classrooms. Deep drawers may hold the disassembled pieces of several children's projects. Sturdy shoe boxes may serve as storage containers slipped onto installed shelving or carefully tucked into a child's desk or cubbyhole. Completed constructions will often necessitate larger spaces. They may be incorporated into a classroom display, a hallway museum or a school library exhibit.

Parallel to the planning process with children, teachers may find it valuable to design a question web to anticipate their own development and decision-making in the orchestration of a project; each will require attention to a different set of details. The teacher may record questions that spin off basic questions of resources, management, and the content. Rather than a sequential enumeration of tasks, this graphic representation shows the connections between areas that are interdependent. For example, questions of time will relate directly to the types of materials that are selected. *With only a forty-five minute period, what materials can be pulled to provide variety without overwhelming the children?* In a similar way, material selection will correspond to techniques. *If we put out burlap, how many children will already know how to use a needle and thread?* In turn, technical skills become a consideration as the teacher timetables opportunities for instruction.

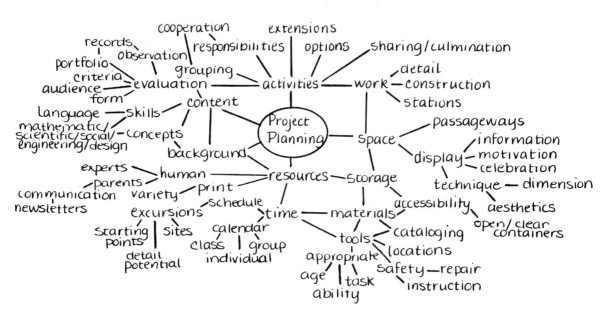

Each of these elements may be turned into a number of questions to assist teachers in planning engineering experiences. For example, resources, time, calendars: How will using individual calendars be introduced? What is the role of negotiation in establishing personal timelines? What dates must be "fixed"? Who will review the calendars, and at what points? Where will the calendars be located?

Dear Parents,

As part of our solids, liquids, and gases unit, our fifth-grade students designed a device that transports water in a solid state. The challenge was to keep the water from changing to a liquid. Students had to have a knowledge of the characteristics of solids and liquids, melting point, volume of space occupied by solids and liquids, effects of different materials as insulators, and the insulating effects of air inside their containers. The students used math skills of measurement and geometry.

Throughout project work the teacher may find it advantageous to make connections with parents. Newsletters alert parents to the activities taking place, to the concepts and skills being developed, and to the materials that can be collected from home and the community. Letters from children to their parents can provide a more personal view into a design experience. Children may write about their project, how they are progressing, and what assistance they might need from their parents. Specific statements can draw parent attention to one particular aspect and help form the direction for a parent-child conversation.

Parents, then, become partners through an awareness of classroom experience and are able to involve the children in relevant follow-up discussions. Parent questions show that the child's work is important and assist the child in articulating their understanding, allowing new questions and expertise to surface.

The management of classroom engineering activities requires thoughtful planning and the desire to take instructional risks. Effective elements of prior practice are brought forward in future modifications. Choreographing this "flow" of a design experience, then, necessitates seeing and building upon connections among curriculum, instructional strategies, and the child's world. The teacher recognizes that the child's development of skills and concepts relies upon exploring interrelationships found, applied, and analyzed in holistic experience.

Connections

Engineering experiences for children may range from a brief modeling of technique to the child's own inquiry within a thematic framework. Challenges may be designed to assist children in understanding concepts within a topic, to embellish a story with props, or to contribute concrete experience in a content area. Community-based field excursions and current events may also offer exciting impetus for a classroom challenge. These entry points, or contexts, represent potential connections for integrating design technology experiences into the required curriculum.

Themes are used as umbrellas for collections of concepts, providing the context for learning processes. Processes, in turn, support the learning of the concepts. Using the Industrial Revolution as an example, this topic would encompass many areas of study. Specifically, mass production could be examined through researching the factories and machine technology during that time. Children involved in design technology project work might select a variety of machines to investigate and then create working models. They would encounter science concepts such as work, force, energy, friction, mass, acceleration, and simple machines. Such first-hand experience provides opportunities to learn and practice a variety of processes. The children may uncover relevant questions of materials and aesthetics. They may link new understandings with an appreciation for invention and its societal consequences within a larger historical context.

In another historical theme, Onward to Oregon, children re-enacted the westward movement through a simulation which began with the construction of Conestoga wagons, broad-wheeled covered wagons drawn by horses. The challenge in this project was to create a replica of the wagons, including rotating axles, a pivoting steering mechanism, and a canvas top.

Working with the confined space of their wagon, the builders also struggled with the list of necessities they would include for their trek. Teams researched supplies available in that period of history, the preservation of food, and quantity of supplies needed for the westward journey. This brought home for the children, in a concrete way, the plight and challenges which faced early settlers. The design technology experience provided a context for children to relate to the human condition in a past era.

Topics in the curriculum provide contexts for concept development. In simple machines children work with creating movements by integrating systems discussed in *Engineering*. Cams, for example, are off-centered wheels that produce vertical movement. They can also be modified to produce diagonal and horizontal movement. In the context of toys children encounter early childhood playthings that use cams to create enticing motion. Even though cams are commonplace, the innerworkings of a cam are not understood fully until children are able to physically explore and manipulate the system.

Fifth and sixth graders observed the movement of toys that incorporated cams. Innerworkings were initially covered up and the children were asked to draw what they saw. They carefully documented in their drawing the motions produced in a mechanically-driven animal. This was the motivation for their own designs for "mechanimals."

The children were challenged to sketch what they perceived occurring inside the toy. They were encouraged to talk with each other and test their ideas through further observation. Incrementally the inner mechanism was revealed. The new information either supported their ideas or challenged them to modify their drawings. The sketches later became scale drawings when the young toy-makers designed animals with similar movements. This inductive experience allowed them to think through the possibilities for the design and construction of their own mechanimals.

Mechanimals set a motivating context for applying mathematical skills of measurement, scale drawing, and computation. The project connected a science topic with communication skills of technical writing and collaboration. Mechanimals became the challenge that permitted children to come to grips with the power and function of cams in everyday mechanisms.

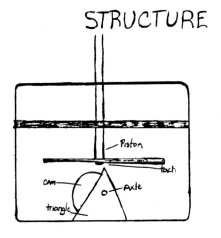

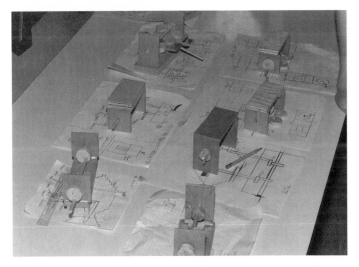

Scale drawings require visualization and a collection of math skills.

Children may vary their designs by the size, shape, number and placement of the cams.

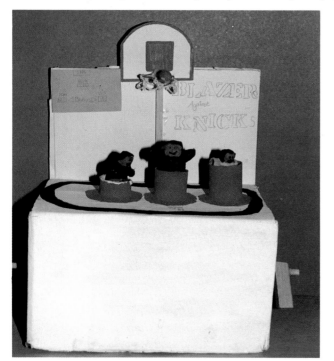 

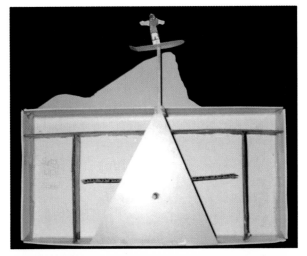

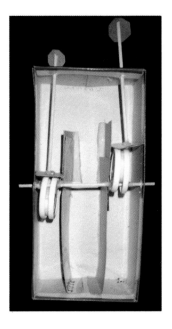

Children solved alignment problems in their cam-driven toys by including spacers.

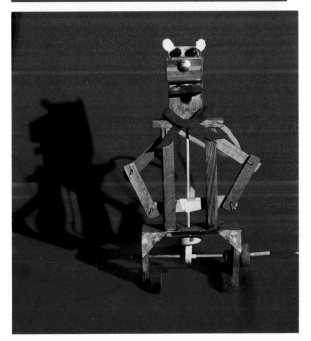

Teachers incorporated the use of cams into more complex movements.

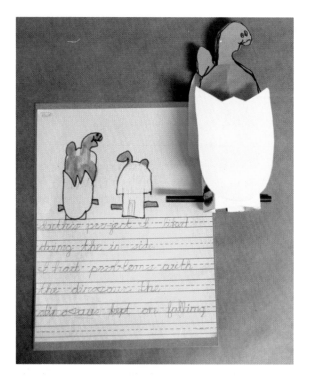

Earlier work in wood by older children was adapted for younger children by using milk cartons, dowels, and cardboard cams. Younger children, also capable of scale drawings, apply appropriate math and visualization skills in planning their pop-up toys. Technical writing focuses on the design and construction process, inherent challenges, and the children's solutions.

The following question chart forecasts the type of inquiries that may assist children, at any age level, in planning. This format, just as a similar question web presented in *Choreography*, comes from class discussions, questions the children pose before work begins, and continued conversations and questions once work is underway.

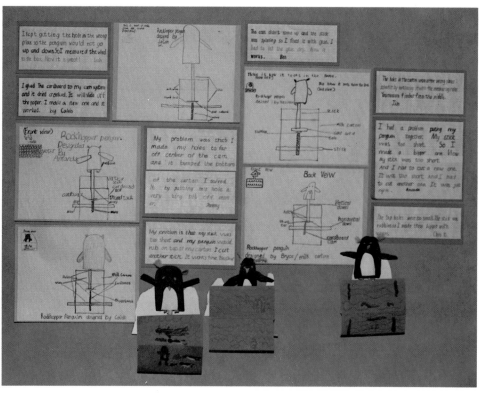

MECHANIMALS

Cam — What is it? How does it work? What can it do? What are the essential features? What materials are appropriate for cam construction? How is it operated? What is the relationship between the size/shape of the cam and the movement of the piston? What is the relationship between the placement of the crankshaft and distance of the piston movement? How does the speed of the axle rotation affect the movement? What is the role of gravity? How can we compensate if gravity is not part of the design? What possibilities would require more than one cam?

Structure — How can the mechanical workings be encased? Can the mechanics be camouflaged or incorporated in the animal? How can the structure be made stronger?

Animal — Which animal movements could be controlled by a cam? What qualities of the animal can be displayed in the construction?

Aesthetics — What materials would add texture to the animal's body? What colors and markings would be attractive and appropriate for the animal? What elaboration can be added to suggest an environment? What details or graphics can be incorporated? How can the planning, construction, and reflection be displayed attractively?

The construction of Mechanimals may be included in the themes Toys, Simple Machines, or Animals.

Literature establishes an imaginative setting for carrying out design technology projects. Props are designed to involve the participants in bringing to life a story through physically creating the set, characters, and mood. For example, teachers in a workshop gained an appreciation for the connection between literature and design experiences through reading *Grandfather Twilight*, a children's book. After hearing the story, the teachers brainstormed a list of key items that were significant for the retelling of the story. They combined ideas and eliminated others. Teams formed and selected one item to be constructed, integrating at least two engineering systems. This became a technological contribution to the re-enactment of the story, one piece of a larger effort.

As children develop their own literary pieces, technology may be applied to enrich the presentation of their writing. In displays or books, children may include the technology of pop-ups and moveable parts. This adds excitement to the original work and becomes a supportive format to enhance its meaning.

Field excursions into the community offer a context for building awareness of local events and sites. 7- and 8-year-olds in Stephanie's class took the opportunity to watch the preparation of land for the construction of new buildings. The children watched the earth movers dig, lift, and transport the soil. They returned to their classroom eager to begin work on their own designs for moving earth. Observational drawings of the tractors linked the field trip to classroom investigations.

A walking tour of the town of Gladstone provided Nancy's youngsters with an opportunity for local map-making and observational drawing of the community buildings. The 6- and 7-year-old surveyors worked in teams with parent volunteers, discussing building features and uses. Back in the classroom the children turned their sketches into a three-dimensional town, complete with emergency vehicles and road signs.

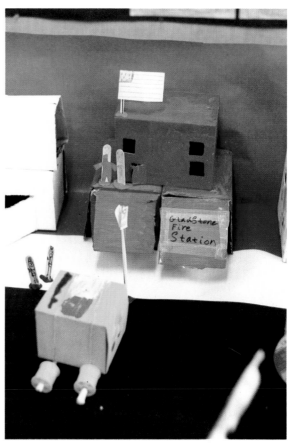

A trip into the city to a carousel museum may furnish first-hand observation of the carousel's circular motion coupled with the vertical movement of the horses. Inquiry starts with this type of exposure to an exciting event. The children may choose to create merry-go-rounds, working in a range of complexity from simple platform rotation to using the downward movement of the horse pole to create levered leg movements.

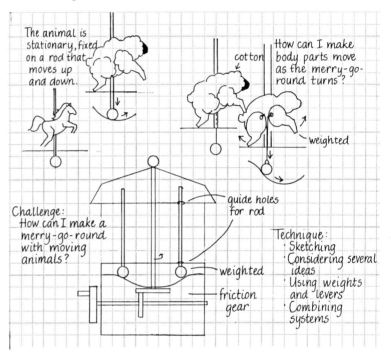

Visiting a local science and technology center, children and teachers interact with a wide variety of exhibitry demonstrating scientific and technological innovations. On one trip to a science center children experimented with a trajectory device in which they estimated the angle of projection and attempted to catch a soft foam ball. Later, in the classroom, children designed catapults that launched chalked tennis balls to accurately hit a target. The chalk left a mark precisely where the target was hit. The children used calibrations on the catapult frame to gauge the anticipated distance. They took data and organized it to find patterns. In building generalizations, the children balanced the relationship of angle, distance, and force.

In the 1920s physicists, led by Heisenberg and Bohr, came to realize that the world is not a collection of separate objects but rather appears as a web of relations between the various parts of a unified whole.

Fritjoh Capra, Uncommon Wisdom: Conversations with Remarkable People

Exciting investigations can also begin at the zoo. Transporting animals, creating feeding systems, replicating movements and sounds, and building habitats are a sampling of design projects. Although design has direct links to physical science and mathematics, it also has notable connections to the biological sciences.

> *...the earth worm became a challenge to one child, "Can I make a model that can expand and contract just like an earth worm?" A wood louse and his armoured plating came out of plastic and brass pin fasteners, "Can I make a shell that curls up and opens out?*
>
> *Andrew Raven*

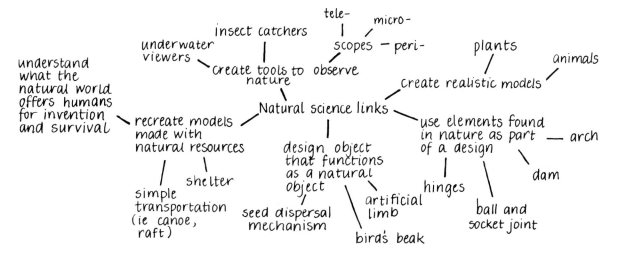

Current events supply rich opportunities for investigation. Bill, an intern teacher working with 9- and 10-year olds in a fourth-grade classroom, shared a particular affection for Alaska with his class. Through his expressed interest and stories about Alaskan natural history, the children became concerned about the devastating effect of the Valdez oil spill of 1989. Focusing on the long-term environmental effects and clean-up efforts, they raised questions that helped Bill design a simulation: *What happened to the animals that were caught in the oil? Why does the clean-up take so long? How will they get the oil off the beaches? How do they get the oil out of the water? Will the birds come back?*

Bill brought in newspaper clippings and first-person accounts of the tragedy. He read them to the children, launching them into an experience planned to help them unravel a number of issues. *In times of crisis people rely on the most recent and accessible forms of technology. Human responses are often shaped by preparedness. And, technological advances respond to needs, often under pressure.* In recreating the immediacy of the crisis, he warned the children that he wasn't going to provide the organization or the answers to their upcoming challenge; after all, the Alaskans had no warning of the accident. *How can you remove the oil from the water and prevent it from reaching the beach?*

The children stared in amazement as Bill poured motor oil into a large tub filled with water piled with sand at one end. The patterns of water and oil were mesmerizing. One boy reminded the group of their challenge and the children quickly set off to gather materials for their hastily-made oil skimmers. Bill unobtrusively moved to another container and released more oil. Several minutes passed before the class noticed the new oil spill which demanded immediate attention, as well.

The whole class headed for the "new spill". They were responding to initial shock and pressure to alleviate a crisis without strategizing. This lack of organization and direction in addressing the challenge made their attempts less effective. Soon realizing that someone needed to attend to the first spill, a team returned to the original site. The children then responded by stationing themselves at various spills and dividing the labor while Bill poured more oil.

The young environmental engineers tried using several materials for their make-shift prototypes. One group designed a metal-handled styrofoam skimmer to collect the oil. Others built plastic-wrap dams to contain black sludge. As a team found a more effective tool or process, neighboring groups were informed of the progress by self-proclaimed reporters.

> *...students should be introduced to scientific subject-matter and be initiated into facts and laws through acquaintance with everyday social applications. Adherence to this method is not only the most direct avenue to understanding of science itself but as the pupils grow more mature it is also the surest road to the understanding of the economic and industrial problems of present society.*
>
> *John Dewey,*
> *Experience and Education*

> *I think intelligence cannot develop without content. Making new connections depends on knowing enough about something in the first place to be able to think of other things to do, of other questions to ask, which demand the more complex connections in order to make sense of it all. The more ideas a person already has at his disposal, the more new ideas occur, and the more he can coordinate to build up still more complicated schemes.*
>
> *Eleanor Duckworth, The Having of Wonderful Ideas*

At the close of the simulation, the class gathered to discuss their experience. In reflecting on the crisis and their parallel response to it, children noticed how they were unprepared for an environmental disaster of this magnitude. They began to develop empathy and greater understanding for those who were involved in the "real-life" drama in Prince William Sound. This conversation became the springboard for developing more sophisticated approaches to possible future spills, knowing that initial attempts fell far short of meeting the challenge effectively.

In creating a rubric, as discussed in *Choreography*, the children were able to move beyond their present achievements to develop more elaborate and complex structures to contain and collect the oil. The children examined their prototypes and shared ideas for combining the most effective features. Work resumed as they set off to improve the technology that may be needed for similar occurrences in the future. Working towards more effective solutions gives children a chance to extend their learning, breaking conceptual barriers and celebrating their ability to make a difference.

Challenges extending from children's interests and classroom needs are also legitimate connections to school curriculum. Gail's 9- and 10-year olds encountered a real classroom challenge. They had spent days creating puppet heads, characterizations, and story lines as part of their literature program. As rehearsals neared, the children discovered that the school's puppet stage was too small to meet their needs.

To address the problem, the group held a class meeting and discussed the elements they would incorporate in a new theater. They also developed a list of things they would need to know in order to construct such a stage. Teams designed and submitted plans to the class. Later the children discussed the desirable features of each and integrated these effective elements into one class plan.

A cardboard refrigerator carton served as the starting point and was reinforced with wood braces. The children measured and cut the stage opening, added an arm rest for comfort, and developed a lighting system. They also devised a roller curtain that raised and lowered on a pulley that locked in place with a multi-level hooking mechanism.

What Characteristics Do We Want for the Stage?

1. A large, wide opening
2. An arm rest
3. A stage front or shelf ledge
4. More room for people in back
5. Less distance to the stage opening
6. Curtain to hide people
7. Decorated and painted attractively
8. A method for hanging design backgrounds
9. A draw system for stage front curtain
10. Spotlights or colored lights
11. Special effects space between stage and background
12. Stage height high enough to stand behind

What Do We Need to Know?

1. How will we make it strong?
2. How will we connect material?
3. How wide does it need to be?
4. How tall does it need to be?
5. How will we measure accurately?
6. What materials do we have? What do we need to get?
7. How do we use some of the tools?
8. Where will we get the materials we need?
9. What method will we use to give everyone a chance to work?

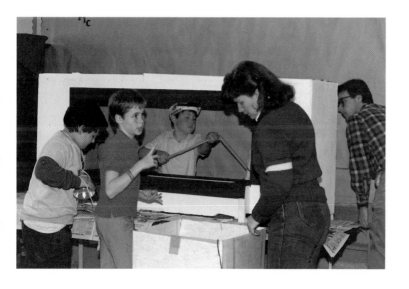

Gail realized the potential of the children's interest in a problem that was relevant to their needs. She was able to seize the opportunity and channel their motivation into activities the children had deemed important. The children shaped their own learning agenda and naturally combined a host of math and science skills in an engineering experience to bolster a language project. In much the same way, a child's interest may be seen as a wonderful opportunity to blend natural inclinations with required curriculum.

Celebration

A carefully-planned child-centered approach to instruction uses natural patterns of learning which channel children's interest in positive ways. It blends dynamically with children's inclinations for discovery and active involvement. A broad range of experiences are offered intentionally; diversity provides avenues for more children to enter into successful learning. Children explore and test limits with enthusiasm in order to uncover connections and discrepancies that bring past and present experiences into a new focus. Teachers begin to see that their children are capable of doing things that were previously thought to be unattainable. For example, the teacher sees in a string toy the motivation, attention, competencies, and joy achieved by a child with learning difficulties who had struggled earlier with any class assignment. Noticing, appreciating, and taking delight in the child's ability to break conceptual and attitudinal barriers, all along the way, *is* the celebration.

A sense of pride throughout the process comes from attending to the many celebration points along the way. Pausing and reflecting on those points of success acknowledge incremental advances, creating enthusiasm and encouraging children to take risks.

The art of attention to success relies upon the teacher's awareness of the numerous dynamics between the children, and between the teacher and children. The teacher balances public acknowledgement and encouragement between wanting to motivate the children and knowing that children need freedom to explore. Sensitivity to this balance comes from knowing the individual child's ability in the context of her social needs and self-esteem. A responsive teacher, then, does not use praise to swing the tide of actions, but to open new options.

Children become sensitive to others in an atmosphere where all children are encouraged to share their successes, where volunteering breakthroughs are not seen as bragging or felt as intimidation. In developing such an atmosphere, the ideal practice is to ask questions rather than allocating praise. Asking children to share information about their projects allows the children to express their own feelings about their work. They judge their actions and results for themselves. For example, exclaiming approval of Jose's use of sandpaper for wheel traction may result in twenty - five replicas with sandpaper-traction wheels. However, *asking* Jose about his wheel design acknowledges his work and allows *him* to point out the features he wants to share, talking about what worked and what didn't. Moreover, Jose is free to change his design or ideas without fearing *dis*approval because no value judgement has been proclaimed by the teacher. His description simply becomes new information in a growing list of options from which the children may choose.

A question will also yield descriptive language about the nature of the process that the children have experienced. *What challenges did you overcome in your design project?* As a child responds to this question, the teacher may listen for subtle and often unknown expressions of success, imbedded in analytical thought rather than a grandstanding posture, embarrassment, or intimidation. The teacher, being sensitive to the child's unique needs, may draw out related successes in a discussion with the class, a small group, or in the more private setting of a conference or journal entry.

Timing is crucial. In identifying successful design resolutions prematurely, the resultant effect of praise is to stop the production of diverse ideas and limit the scope of solutions. Noticed after children have a chance to explore a range of ideas, sharing can provide opportunity for *exchange* of ideas and comparison of results.

Documentation such as early sketches and technical writing, may be shared during their development and at the close of a project. Children may feel a sense of pride as their thinking is given value equal to the value typically reserved for a finished product. Helped to feel successful throughout the process, the child takes pride in her accomplishments, talking about her investment. She has a real purpose for meaningful conversation, experience from which to draw, and a piece that she is proud to share with classmates.

These artifacts, displayed in respectful ways, motivate discussion and inquiry into the processes and products of the design experience. Classroom interaction about a display of a child's work provides reinforcement from peers and a classroom audience for the risk-taking engineer. Young designers are asked to reflect on the inherent challenges and turning points in the project to document and celebrate progressive insights and accomplishments.

Display of children's work becomes a more permanent form of celebration. Effective presentations of children's work highlight areas of study, provide points of inquiry and motivation, set a standard of work quality, establish a child-centered ethos, and capture the uniqueness of a particular group of children and their teacher working together.

Areas of study are recorded through display work, evolving illustrated histories of classroom learning. Children may refer to these displays for information, drawing upon past projects as new topics of investigation are introduced. This type of classroom suggests an exciting learning environment for both adults and children. Visitors entering a classroom that is alive with color and child-created evidence of learning are drawn into the richness of an exciting curriculum. They are provided with useable information for talking with children and for joining in the celebration of their efforts.

> *To display children's work with care and dignity is to celebrate that work. It allows us an alternative way in which we can communicate that our schools are places of warmth and care, interest and beauty, excitement and fascination, learning and growth...to child, teacher, parent and visitor alike.*
>
> *ILEA Teachers' Art Centre*

Classroom exhibitry, collections of interactive models and text created by the children, invite others to participate in a less formal and free choice learning environment. These exhibits celebrate the child as an expert and may become starting points for further investigations. Children take pride in their inventions as classroom curators explain the innerworkings to interested visitors.

Quality of children's work is developed over time. Discussing class-determined criteria, practicing techniques, and modeling, build working patterns for attractive display. Standards may be set directly for neatness and accuracy, whereas, colorful, matted publications require negotiation as children become more skilled at artistic aspects of display. Indirectly, messages of acceptable standards permeate the classroom through the choice and arrangement of children's work. The teacher's practice communicates clearly to adults and children what is valued.

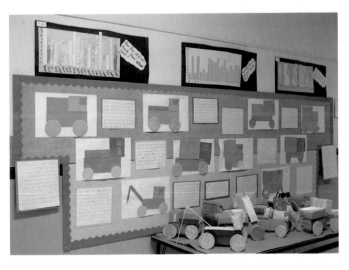

The uniqueness of a classroom is the identifying hallmark of its participants. The interplay of teacher strengths and child energies produces a distinct atmosphere as seen in the arrangement, use, and the decoration of space. The ethos of such an environment suggests an openness and diversity in ways to learn and in what is learned. Evidence of children's work is given obvious significance, demonstrated by placement in the room, careful attention to framing and labeling, and an artistic touch with detail.

To be an effective presentation of children's work, a display is set at a level that draws children's attention and is comfortable to view. It is located in a place that is accessible to children and is appropriately lit. Displays which are intended for more public viewing may require spaces outside the classroom - the entry hall of the school, hallways, and other common areas, such as the school library and cafeteria. More fragile displays may be placed in cases or in protected, out-of-the-way corners. Windows, sills, doorways and ceilings are often neglected spaces. These locations have a variety of features which hold potential for the creative display and celebration of children's work.

Framing written work involves consideration to color, size, and proportion. Color is used to complement and draw out particular features in the child's work. In order to assist children in developing a sense of color use, the teacher takes time with the child to try combinations of mat colors and a variety of border sizes. Matting takes into account the proportions that are required to attractively display work without overwhelming it. The effects are discussed and choices are made based on the match with the specific piece and the larger display. Trimming work can accentuate positive aspects of the work while eliminating unnecessary or detracting space.

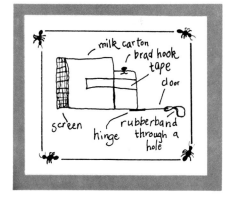

Children may use lined paper underneath blank paper to align their writing for a final presentation. To declare borders around the work, guide lines may also be used in the layout. This guide will inform children of the area intended for their final product while providing space for decorative borders that highlight the work.

The complete presentation of children's work includes careful lettering. Titles, labels, questions, and directions add interest, acknowledgement, and another level of viewer interaction through reading. Writing is appropriately placed at an audience's eye level and is large enough to see. It is attractive and the style supports the subject of the display.

Added artistic touches to design and layout also embellish classroom display. Materials and borders may be used to create a unity in a collection of work. Cascading fabrics tie together two-dimensional and three-dimensional work. Multi-leveled platforms can be created using hidden boxes under cloth to create an interesting effect.

Presentation techniques are designed to catch attention and engage the viewer. Including questions invites interaction, luring children to touch and think. Attention to celebration through display is an integral part of the design technology process, rewarding children's risk-taking and promoting further investigation. As launching points for conversation, key elements in children's work can be celebrated with peers and parents alike and used as springboards for reflection.

Reflection

Teachers and children engaged in reflective evaluation will experiment with criteria, strategies, and formats which are suited to their purpose. In evaluating design experiences a variety of questions and perspectives may be considered. The teacher and the children are closest to the teaching and learning process and possess insights into what is most relevant for their own growth.

Teachers continuously engage in observing, monitoring, and evaluating, informally and formally. Teachers gather information to establish baselines against which progress will be measured. Data is collected informally through sensitive child-watching and more formally through work appraisals and testing. Over time teachers gauge progress relative to criteria. This is based on the teacher's knowledge of child development and what is appropriate for a particular age range. Criteria for a specific child is also related to the teacher's range of experience with other children and that particular child's history. Observations are brought forward in monitoring as the teacher interprets information and looks for patterns. In turn, this leads to making judgments. Understanding the child's needs and strengths, and deciding what information is important to keep and what is important to pursue, the teacher develops aims for and with children.

Reflective evaluation is a cyclic process of observing, monitoring, and evaluating. As seen on page 23 reflection weaves throughout the design technology experience. Teachers are able to evaluate in a contextualized situation elements that are often measured in isolation. In a formal testing situation the attainment of a process, concept, or attitude is often based on the recall of information in isolation. In design technology experiences, teachers are able to witness and document not only the existence of processes, concepts, and attitudes but also their collective power in a problem-solving application.

At times, design technology experiences may blend easily with requirements and record-keeping in the context of the school and district frameworks. Reflection allows teachers to understand that they can meet the curricular needs of children and the specifications of the written curriculum through innovative teaching. Attention to both allows the teacher to ascertain whether children are progressing in the attainment of processes, concepts, and attitudes.

In detailing the match between the written curriculum and selected engineering experiences, the teacher describes the connections as a forecasting exercise. Processes, concepts, and attitudes are anticipated in light of a design experience. At times, these experiences are selected because of the likelihood that certain objectives in the curriculum will be introduced or developed through them. However, in prescribing an experience so tightly that it becomes a straightjacket, teachers may deny opportunities for children to embark on original ideas. This reduces a well-intended educational experience to an excursion of copying the original thought and format of another. When sharing ideas, teachers might listen for possibilities rather than trapping themselves into replicating activities and products that were successful in another situation. It is essential that teachers forecast and reflect matches with a degree of flexibility. Each experience is seen as unique, molded by a particular set of circumstances.

Evaluation information, then, is descriptive of where children are and where they are going, what is known, what is emerging, and what will be developed. At any one point in time, it is simply a snapshot, an abstraction out of a complex system of interactions among people and events. It is a sampling, a record of what is happening in the classroom to be shared with children, parents, teachers, and school officials.

A variety of opportunities for formative evaluation take place throughout the evolution of a particular project. The teacher, engaged in planning an experience, may think about similar past experiences. She will draw upon successful aspects and address concerns that arose to gauge and structure a new starting point. In a similar manner, the child working with a challenge will return to previous experiences and use related aspects to inform and enhance the new piece of work. Throughout the engineering activity, the child and teacher will continue to ask questions, trying new ideas, and applying processes in light of the design requirements. The child actively tackles challenges while the teacher watches for conceptual development and helps the young designer clarify her direction.

Drawing upon an earlier experience of developing a rubric, the child may come to a conference with some notions of criteria for examining her plans. These initial criteria may be reflected upon throughout the formative and summative evaluation phases.

> *The true teacher intuits the level of readiness, then probes, questions, leads.*
> Marilyn Ferguson, The Aquarian Conspiracy

Conferences between the child and teacher are important for establishing a partnership and continuing formative reflection. Early on this may give the child her first opportunity to articulate questions and ideas that form the basis of her project. *What are your ideas? Where did they come from? What problems might occur? What resources will be needed?* Open-ended questions invite her to participate in guided self-reflection. Through careful listening and following the child's lead, the sensitive teacher will ask questions that probe intuitive hunches and illuminate intent. These discussions are critical for uncovering what a child understands and has attempted, and for visualizing further development.

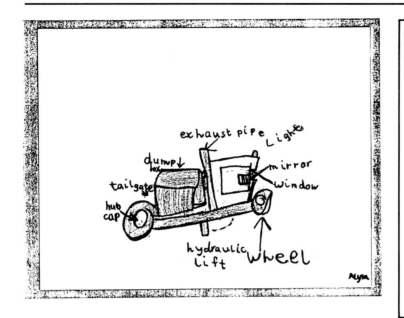

exhaust pipe Lights

dump box

mirror

tailgate

window

hub cap

hydraulic lift wheel

Alysa

Pull Toy
I experimented hundreds of times and then it hit me. I needed to see it while it was working! I put the wings on the outside and the penguin worked.

I pulled down on the string that pulled another string attached to the wings. The brads held it in place so the wings worked.

I learned to be very patient. This could be used to transport things by putting the load in the loop and moving the wings.

I had to think first. I put pieces of paper on to another piece of big paper to plan it. How did we build our trucks? We used cardboard and wood boxes. My truck went five seconds. My truck went 8 square.

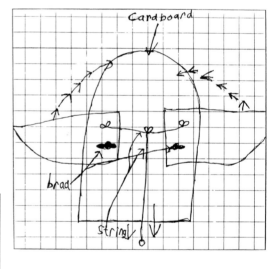

Cardboard

brad

string

Pulley

Front View →

Side View

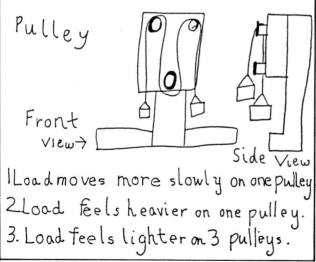

1 Load moves more slowly on one pulley
2 Load feels heavier on one pulley.
3. Load feels lighter on 3 pulleys.

The Pull Toy
I made a Blueprint. I got some string and some brads. Then I got my paper and my scissors. I cut out my shapes. Then I started fiddling with my stuff until I got the right design. And now I pull the string and the ears move.

The holes in the carton were in the wrong places. I solved it by measuring it with the measuring ruler. You measure 4 inches from the middle.
Jim

My problem is that my stick was too short and my penguin would rub on top of my carton. I cut another stick. It works fine. Heather

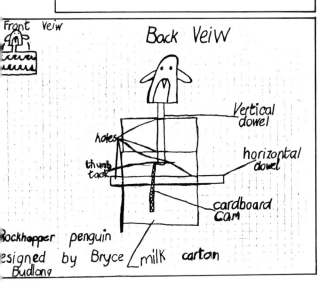

Front Veiw

Back Veiw

Vertical dowel

holes

thumb tack

horizontal dowel

cardboard Cam

Rockhopper penguin designed by Bryce Budlong / milk carton

The top holes were too small. The stick was rubbing, so I made them bigger with scissors.
Chris D.

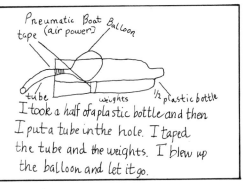

Pneumatic Boat (air power) Balloon
tape
tube   weights   ½ plastic bottle

I took a half of a plastic bottle and then I put a tube in the hole. I taped the tube and the weights. I blew up the balloon and let it go.

tape   hooks

balloon wings   body

My problem on the airplane was the paper clips and the balloon. I had trouble taping the paper clips. I taped the balloon too tight. But I fixed it. The airplane went 109 inches.

How We Made Our Vehicles

First we wrapped boxes. Then we used pieces of dowel for the axles. We used rubber-bands to hold the dowel. We used thread spools for the wheels. We used vinyl tubing to hold the wheels on. We decorated our vehicles. We checked our axles to see if they were straight by running them down a ramp. If the axles weren't on straight our vehicles ran off the side of the ramp.

Learnings logs are valuable as a written format for capturing thoughts that may have been initially expressed in a conference. They provide access to two types of information: the development of the project and the development of the child. Learning logs are written shapshots of the child's ideas at a given point in time. She enters her recent trials, resolutions, and feelings to mark key points in the evolution of her design. Early entries may serve later purposes when projects take unexpected turns. This type of recording is also used by designers, engineers, and scientists as they make notations about their work. Learning logs may also be used as evaluative evidence, highlighting change and growth. Reading the log informs the perceptive teacher of the thought processes and underlying cognitive development.

The learning log allows the teacher and child to communicate personally and privately with concentrated attention, which is more difficult during an action-packed day. The stimulus for entries in the learning log comes from question webs, group discussions, readings, or individual queries. Conference suggestions or questions which emanate from a field excursion also fuel written thoughts. A response may be a simple note of encouragement, a resource offering, or a question intended to spark further consideration.

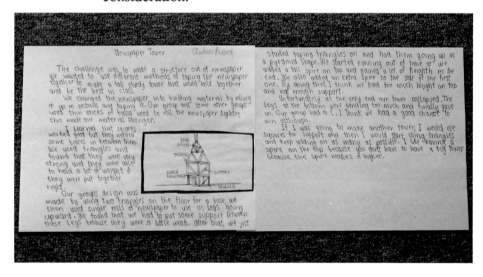

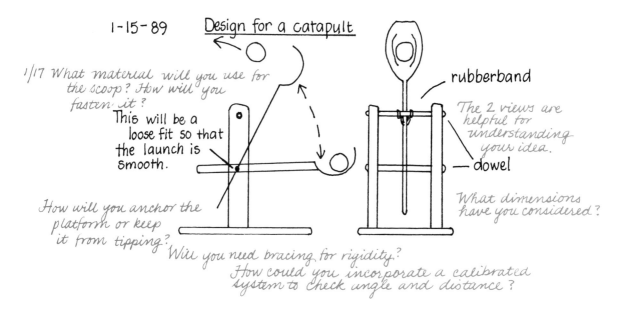

1-15-89   Design for a catapult

1/17 What material will you use for the scoop? How will you fasten it?

This will be a loose fit so that the launch is smooth.

rubberband

The 2 views are helpful for understanding your idea.

— dowel

How will you anchor the platform or keep it from tipping?

What dimensions have you considered?

Will you need bracing for rigidity? How could you incorporate a calibrated system to check angle and distance?

Reflective templates offer versatility for evaluation. Some work is difficult to respond to directly in writing. The work's shape and intricacies require an intermediate format for recording specific points. With this technique, the child replicates her project in its current stage as a basic outline drawing. The size of the drawing paper selected depends on the audience who will critique the work. The child's personal reflections might occur on a standard sized piece of typing paper. Response from larger audiences will require more space. If the piece to be evaluated is two-dimensional-- a plan, print, or display of information, for example --thin paper can be used over the work to trace the major elements. If the work is three-dimensional, the child draws the work, including the most important features. The actual model may accompany the reflective template for inspection.

In responding to a prototype, the evaluation is formative. After examining the piece the child writes her thoughts on the reflective template. She jots notes about points of success, questions, and areas that need further work. She might also consider adaptations. Likewise, the teacher may add comments that provide encouragement and constructive critique. At this stage, notations may include the design idea, structure, and materials, with suggestions for adornment, elaboration, and display.

Working portfolios house the child's collection of work in progress. As the teacher makes notations that help propel the work forward she may add them to an individual's manila folder which is the gathering point of her work. The child will encounter the teacher suggestions as she begins the next work session.

> *...the evaluation of design and technology activities in an educational context involves more than simply the evaluation of the end product...we are concerned to probe the quality and development of pupils' thinking through the interaction between the mind and the hand and therefore we scrutinize the design folio for evidence that helps us to evaluate both the process and the product of that interaction. The evidence is naturally in the form of sketches, notes, models etc. that represent the pupils' attempts to engage their creative speculations with the material world.*
> *Department of Education and Science, Design and Technological Activity: A Framework for Assessment*

All of these strategies - conferences, learning logs, reflective templates, and working portfolios - may be equally as valuable at the conclusion of a project for developing a summative evaluation. At this point, the information may reflect the rubric criteria and individually selected criteria. Conference questions and learning log entries may detail a review of the process and the satisfaction with the results. *What problems occurred? How were they resolved? What new problems resulted? What might you change?* Using a reflective template, comments might focus on details of accuracy, durability, and craftsmanship. Furthermore, the template can be used for other children or adults to record their critique.

The teacher may find it helpful to create a working portfolio or notebook of projects. Initial plans and modifications, lists of materials and resources, schedules, calendars, and time requirements may be included in this project book. It also may be beneficial to include prototypes, samples of children's work, and photographs for referral. Reviewing and working from this collection, the teacher may incorporate additional ideas and try different combinations of instructional variables, leading to new challenges.

Leading Out

In thinking about engineering challenges for children, teachers balance considerations presented by children and by the school curriculum. The extent to which a design problem is open or closed falls along a continuum and represents a negotiation of these diverse needs. The continuum is defined by a number of key questions and the range of responses to these questions.

Each design experience merits consideration of the full range of the questions found on the following pages. The interplay between the responses defines countless possibilities and characterizes the project as more open or closed. The goal is a balance of diverse experience over time. This balance requires a match among intent, needs, and the abilities of the children and teacher. Different combinations of open and closed features produce a vast array of options with specific advantages tailored to identified instructional needs. Each combination offers its own rewards and limitations. However, when all options of a project are routinely set at extreme ends of each continuum, thinking is limited.

Softened by other characteristics of more open challenges, the form of a product may be prescribed and children will still bring individuality to the process. In following a pattern many different questions will be raised. With flexibility, modifications may be made and interim steps may vary. The limitation of time, materials, and tools in an isolated challenge set by a teacher may point up the wide *variety* of possibilities that can stem from such limitations. Some combinations may be helpful in focusing the children's attention on a particular technique or material, or serve as a common base from which to discuss the design and construction process.

Design Technology Challenges
Open - Closed Continuum

What is the context of the task?

Natural childhood context   School-based curriculum

|_____|_____|

Child-centered topic work

Who sets the challenge?

Child-identified   Teacher-identified

|_____|_____|

Child-selected from a range of given
options or negotiated with the teacher

What materials and tools are available?

Wide range of choice   Limited range

|_____|_____|

Some selection

Who selects the materials?

Child-selected   Teacher-selected

|_____|_____|

Negotiation based on need,
availability, and substitution

What form will the result take?

Child-designed   Pattern
|_____|_____|
Variations on a pattern

What steps will be taken?

Discovered   Direct instruction
|_____|_____|
Guided

Who sets the criteria for the challenge?

Child   Teacher
|_____|_____|
Negotiated between
child and teacher

Who evaluates the process and result?

Child   Teacher
|_____|_____|
Child-teacher partnership

How much time is available?

Determined by child   Prescribed time unit
|_____|_____|
Negotiated according to task,
child's needs, and availability

On the other hand, the child's cognitive skills are more likely to develop when the openness of free play is tempered with supportive adult guidance. Children may set the context and resources, moving in and out of a storyline or plan according to surfacing criteria and satisfaction with the results. Options for further investigation become available through the teacher's involvement. Confidence with materials, tools, and the design process is expanded through a concerted attempt to build on previous experiences.

This series of continua, then, provide elements of a formula for increasing a teacher's instructional options and developing original activities. It provides a scale with which to check for plans appropriately matched to intent and a long-term balance.

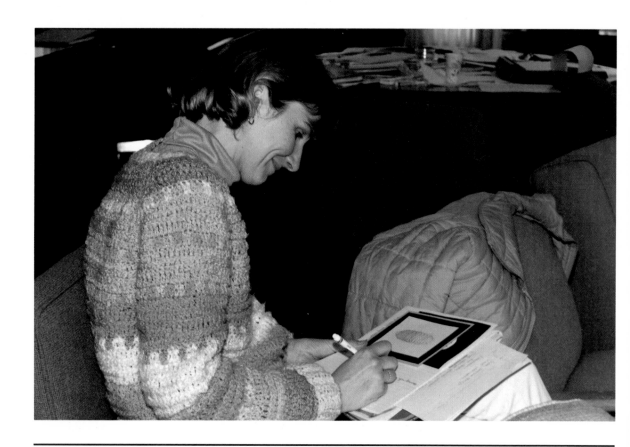

Beginnings

8- to 10-year-olds in Judy and Sid's classrooms worked on designing and making their own moving winter ornaments. The introductory scenario was the same for each class. The teachers showed the models of "jumping" snowmen and dolls. The children drew the ornamental casings they could see and noted the limb movements.

Each child added the innerworkings suggested by the movements. *"How do you think this works?" "Draw what you think you would see if you could see through the casings".* The children consulted with each other to challenge and gain insights, and to check a number of perceptions.

The teachers moved about the room asking the children to explain their designs. Many children used their own bodies to show how they thought the movements were produced. With a finger firmly pressed into his shoulder, one boy moved his arm up and down to act out his understanding of a pivot. Another youngster used a strip of paper held down on the desk by a pencil point. Moving the strip up and down she talked about the pivot and tentatively explored the placement of an imaginary string on the upper arm that would move the limb when it was pulled.

Additional hints were provided for the children to assimilate in their drawings. The teachers showed the children the models more closely. They had the opportunity to look at the spacings, the attachments, and the string placement. The children revised their ideas with the new information or proclaimed satisfaction with their original drawings.

Excited by the moving model, the children were ready to make their own. *"What were the most important features?"*

"What could be changed?" "What other things might have a similar movement?" Having listed many options they moved to other considerations. *"How big should it be?" "What materials were available and how can they be used?"*

Each child produced a pattern. Some consulted resource books. One 10-year-old found the need to use an encyclopedia to make a recognizable deer. Patterns were cut and traced onto more durable cardstock. Some children experimented with thicker cardboard to increase strength. Others, realizing their scissors were no match for the denser material, increased material strength by cutting a second set separately and gluing the like pieces together to double the thickness.

Children also explored the placement of the string on the appendage for the most movement. They also found that extreme movements presented a challenge. A couple of girls worked out the movements for a toybox lid lifting and exposing toys. They found it necessary to add a "stopper" to keep the lid from falling backward.

One boy found that cutting the spacers a specific size presented a measurement problem. *"How can 1 centimeter be cut from a straw measuring 12 centimeters?"* With teacher assistance he was able to develop an efficient strategy for moving the straw along a ruler, reducing its corresponding measurement 1 cm to create a 1 cm "overhang" that could be snipped off the end.

The children marked their designs for the quick-drying glue applied by the teacher using a hot glue gun. Some children assembled their pieces before the final encasement and found it necessary to make some adjustments. The arms of several snowmen would not return to a "resting" position. *"What was the problem?"* *"How could it be solved?"*

"How could the solution be incorporated into the design?" The children wrestled with this and discovered that the weight of those short arms had to overcome the force of the weighty pull-strings. The effect of additional weight was tested by placing paperclips on the arms at the end opposite the pivot, or fulcrum. The solution took two directions. Several children exchanged the string for thread. Others increased the weight at the end of the arms by adding pom-poms, flowers, brooms, or mittens. These elaborative details added uniqueness and character to similar designs while also resolving a problem.

There was a busy hum throughout the classroom as children wrestled with the challenges they identified and finished their work. The intensity was punctuated intermittently with shared excitement about each successful accomplishment extending from this initial experience. Several girls created a two and a half foot snowman with moveable arms. One mother later talked about the enthusiasm the activity generated at home; her child passed the winter break creating ornaments for family gifts.

Children wrote in their journals about the experience. *What successes did you have? What was the most difficult part? What did you do to solve the problems you encountered? How did you feel about the process and your finished ornament? If you were to do it again, what would you change? What did you learn?*

Sharon, a teacher involved in designing and constructing her own ornament, discovered a technique for solving a gluing problem. The glue continued to run down the straw pivot joints and impede the appendage movement. She decided to apply the glue to the "free" side rather than the straw spacers. That required glue-spot accuracy. Pressing the straws onto an inkpad and then onto the free side provided marks on which to dab the glue.

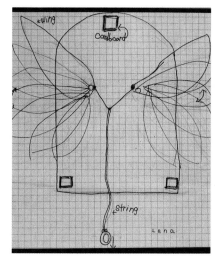

In Helen and Cathy's classes, 7- and 8-year-olds drew bird shapes and made winged versions of the pull-toys. They drew their plans on graph paper and used those plans as blueprints for their constructions.

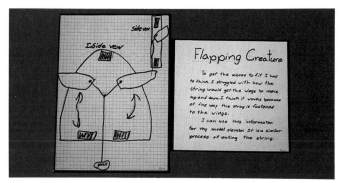

In other classrooms, the "ornaments" were made to portray story characters. Others added a stick handle and worked the arm and leg strings separately, creating a number of movements to act out the storylines created by children.

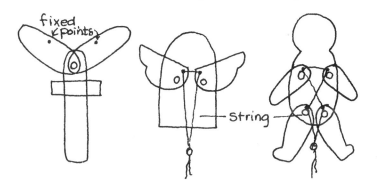

A variety of mechanisms may control similar movement

* * *

After reading Mrs. Minnetta's Carpool to 7- to 8- year-olds in Helen's classroom, children set the challenge to design and construct their own cars. Using the story as a motivating context, the children were soon involved in their first design experience. They decided the cars would need to move down a ramp and should have moveable parts. Children were then asked to investigate questions that came to mind about designing and making a car. Thoughts came together in the form of a question web, and patterns in the children's thinking began to surface.

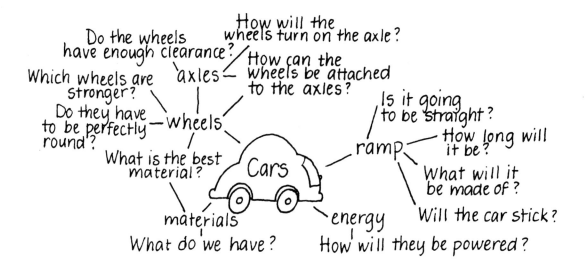

With the challenge clarified, and initial design considerations discussed, the children set off on their tasks. Cardboard boxes served as chassis in some designs, whereas cardboard corners were useful for other chassis made of 1/2 x 1/2 inch wood scraps. Wheels were fashioned from cardboard, styrofoam, combinations of pipe insulation and cotton reels, and, in some cases, the plastic lids of fast-food drinks containers. Materials selection and use became important as children discovered that plastic lids made good wheels when used with cardboard rather than wood chassis. Pipe insulation and cotton reels seemed to work well with the heavier wood construction.

Helen found it helpful to circulate among the students during the work period. Often times she would assist a child with a design or engineering difficulty by providing another pair of hands, offering an encouraging smile, or proposing a well-timed question to lead a child closer to an emerging concept. One student, however, appeared to present instructional challenges of a different kind.

Chai Ian, an 8-year-old from Thailand, with limited English language skills, had been in the United States for only a short period of time. He was reserved and displayed little curiosity or enthusiasm in class and often seemed uninterested in classroom activities. Previous class work was predominantly dependent on verbal and written communication and touched little of his own experience. Helen wondered if Chai Ian's response to this type of activity would be different. Her instructional questions focused her observations as she watched Chai Ian begin to design his car: *In what ways might his withdrawal be due to cultural differences? Did he understand the challenge? How might his limited English language ability influence his understanding of the challenge and his approach? Would he feel free to try alternate ideas? Would he continue his design through to a finished rendering?*

Chai Ian seemed to have a basic understanding of the challenge. With some hesitation he began to collect a variety of materials to design his car. With agile fingers he first developed a cardboard tissue-box chassis, and then in a moment's time, he decided to use a styrofoam tray. The excitement and joy was growing.

Thomas, a nearby student, was having trouble getting his wheels to rotate as Chai Ian offered a gentle suggestion. Pointing to the sides of the tray he showed Thomas where the wheels were rubbing against the chassis. This moment of collaboration seemed to provide a new social connection for a child who had previously remained aloof.

> *To young children the world is one. They are active, they are curious, they want to explore and experience. They run from one part of the field of experience to another quite regardless of the fences we put round what we call subjects. They do not regard them because they do not see them, and if we insist on recognition we simply impede their progress and retard their learning.*
>
> *Christian Schiller*

Chai Ian began to test his car on the inclined plane provided by the teacher. It worked! With a broad grin revealing his strong sense of accomplishment, he began to see more challenges to embellish his design. A balloon and a piece of tubing soon became a stimulus for further experimentation and a power source. Colorful markings identified his car as a unique accomplishment.

Soon other children gathered around to observe the experiments in process. Chai Ian repeatedly demonstrated the operability and beauty of his design. Though his sharing was through demonstration and not verbal communication, the other children celebrated his success and borrowed ideas to use in their own plans.

The next day Chai Ian took his car to his ESL (English as a Second Language) class. Given an opportunity to share his creation in that setting, Chai Ian began a lengthy description of his design and how it was developed. While demonstrating and describing his car, other children asked questions, which were followed by *more* detailed explanations. During the sharing process Chai Ian needed to make additional changes and fix parts of the car that would not stand up to the already frequent use. With previously unseen persistence, Chai Ian modified and corrected his new-found challenges.

* * *

Spring arrived and so did the ants. The children in Barbara's first grade class were naturally drawn to the microscopes that focused their attention on these common critters. The class developed a web of ant information and questions. They used reference sources, observed natural ant colonies, and constructed an ant farm to gather evidence to support their ideas and answer their own inquiries. These 6- and 7-year-olds wrote ant study books, drew ant hill cross-section maps of the ant farm, and made observational drawings. Word lists grew as records of body parts, descriptive words, ant movements, and locations created a cache for factual and impressionistic writing.

Early drawings revealed misconceptions about ant anatomy. Many children showed the three leg pairs attached to separate body sections-- head, thorax, and abdomen. Careful observation and discussion helped the children realize that all three pairs were attached to the thorax. The children cut paper body parts and arranged them according to their new understanding. This became the plan that guided the three-dimensional creation of ant marionettes with moveable and controllable parts.

Ants
All of their legs are on the thorax. The queen has wings. So does the drone. They have soldiers too. They can carry 250 times their weight. They work all the time. We have an ant farm in our classroom.

Children formed the head, thorax, and abdomen from globs of wadded newspaper wound with masking tape and papier mâché. The legs were bent characteristically from pipe cleaners. Challenges came in connecting the body parts to allow movement and in stringing the marionettes for easy manipulation. One effective solution was the development of links, or joints, imbedding paper clips in adjoining ends of the papier mâché masses. Strings suspended the ant head and abdomen from one chopstick and the thorax from another. Discussions often centered on the stringing of the ants. *How long should the strings be? If this one is this long, how long should this string be? What would happen if all three strings were on separate chopsticks or only on one chopstick? How short is too short? Can the string be too long? How can I keep the strings from tangling?*

Adjustments were made in string lengths and placements as the puppeteers practiced maneuvering their pets. The children's final drawings and writings reflected new anatomical information that was discovered and reinforced through the active process of design and construction. The fit between biological concepts of form and movement and similar physical science concepts allowed the children to explore and make connections between seemingly diverse areas of science.

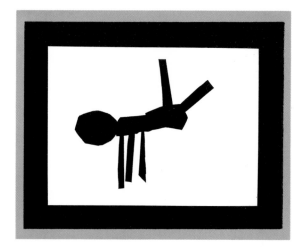
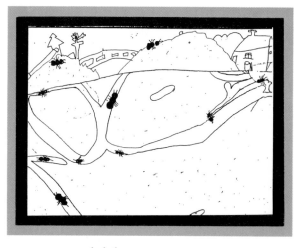

* * *

Bridges became the interdisciplinary topic for exploration by 6- and 7-year-olds in Barbara and Connie's classrooms. The children recalled their experiences with traffic and foot bridges and set about designing simple replicas. Working with ten pennies, each team of children "purchased" construction paper and tape, calculating their coffer's balance along the way.

The bridge builders found that rolling the construction paper formed stronger columns on which to position their roadways. Longer bridges required longer lengths of construction paper and more columns for stability. Shorter, wider columns seemed to bend less and, therefore, provided more strength for the roadway than taller, thin

Our class made a big bridge. We put two girders on our bridge. We had to make it sturdy. We tested it with our cars.

columns. The children tested their bridge constructions by running toy cars across them and sensing the weaknesses. Modifications were made by propping up flimsier road sections with more columns or adding another layer of construction-paper pavement. At the conclusion of the project, children wrote up their engineering reports and calculated their expenses.

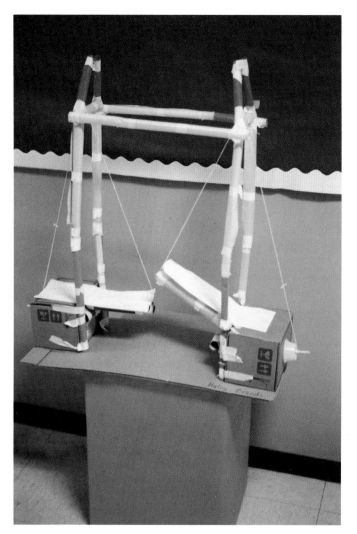

Springing from this earlier style of bridge, Barbara's children built a class model of a suspension bridge. Connie's children investigated drawbridges. Forming companies, they drafted and built models that opened and closed by turning wheels and winding string, raising the bridge crossing. Hallway displays provided interactive exhibitry for passers by.

* * *

A challenge was set for 12- to 14-year-olds to construct, from a limited supply of balsa, individual bridges that would bear as much weight as possible. Bridges were designed to withstand weight that descended to a makeshift ravine. Tests were conducted by placing weights incrementally in a bucket attached to the lower level of the bridge. As breaking points neared, successively smaller weights were added to determine precise measurements and to discern differences between bridge holding capacities. Calculations were made and charted to show holding capacity to bridge weight ratios.

* * *

Toys became the study for 11-and 12-year-olds in Mary's classroom. Children designed toys that were simple, safe and attractive. Considerable time was spent in the development of workable prototypes prior to investment in more sophisticated tools and materials. In creating prototypes, the children explored material properties that would respond in a similar manner as the intended material of the final model. Mechanical systems were investigated for their value in producing movements required in the design. Consideration was given to size, shape, and proportion as documented in rough drawings. Accuracy and aesthetics became increasingly significant as intention and construction merged.

An initial draft of a cat dipping his paw in a fishbowl was constructed using tag board, straws and glue. Realizing that the finely-detailed prototype was much too small for easy manipulation, the young designer changed the scale for a larger, final rendition. The latter version, made of styrofoam, wood, and cardboard, proved to be a much more satisfactory size.

One girl began her baby-and-crib toy by incorporating a modified cam system. She discovered that a simple vertical piston-and-cam system is gravity dependent or requires a retraction device. Applying this knowledge to a horizontal design meant concealing rubberbands that were necessary to pull back the horizontal piston. The piston was designed to move the baby's hands and bottle to and from its mouth. Hiding it was not successful. Scrapping the original draft, she used a rod, covered by a blanket, to pull the baby's hands and bottle forward. This raised the baby's head which was connected to the bottle with a rubberband. Another rubberband, extended to the base of the crib from the head, provided sufficient tension to return the baby to a resting position when she released the rod.

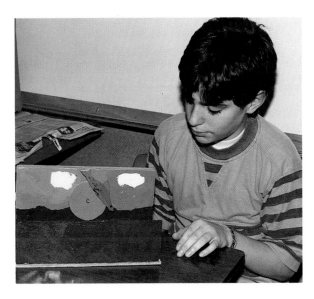

The early draft of a dolphin swimming through waves was worked out using a construction kit. The toy designer incorporated a gearing system that would rotate the dolphin as he turned a crank. The final display was carefully crafted of wood and cardboard to meet his own specifications.

* * *

Robots became a project focus for 6- and 7-year olds in Connie and Jennifer's class. The young designers first drew the robots they planned to create from a collection of boxes of various shapes and sizes. The children selected and wrapped the boxes that best matched their original plans. They connected the boxes using brass brads, tape, sticks, and rubber bands, creating moveable joints in the robotic limbs. The robots' arms and legs were strung with string and fastened to chop sticks to produce controlled motion. Buttons, yarn, ribbon, and foil adorned the life-size playmates.

Soon, robot buddies were "walking" and "talking" throughout the room as their animators created delightful chatter. This gave the children ample time to experiment with conversational language, often in robotic monotone. The children then wrote their exchanges in different colored markers, signaling change of speakers, at which point Connie used the occasion to introduce quotation marks.

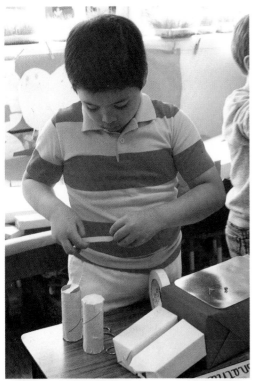

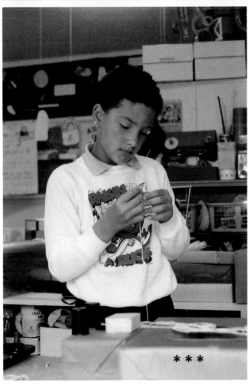

* * *

The circus wagons spun out! With roll-back rubber band-powered wagons, the challenge for 6- and 7-year-olds was to keep them traveling in a straight line. The children pulled their wagons backwards on the ground, each one winding a rubberband around an axle. The rubber band was attached to one axle, fixed to a point on the bottom of the chassis.

Initially, the wagons were too light and the wheels simply spun. Several children found that adding weight to the chassis slowed the wheel rotation. Using varying amounts of clay, the children experimented with the needed quantity to keep the wagons going in a straight line as fast as possible. When just the right amount was determined, the clay ballast was formed into animals for the wagon cage.

The teacher understood that the children were working in the early stage of developing a connection between mass and friction. Heavier objects in the circus wagon created more friction on the wheels which caused it to move slowly. If the objects were too light, there was not enough friction and the wheels spun without moving the vehicle. The children worked with the relationships in order to discover a balance among the mass of the vehicle, the needed friction for wheel traction, and the power of the rubberband system.

Children also designed pop-up writings using library books as models. Published pop-up cages were exhibited along with paper acrobats and ceramic clowns.

Follow me, everyone! Follow me to see the zebra!

The zebra sleeps with his eyes open. He has a great big cage in the circus. There is a clown by his cage laughing at him. He has black stripes.

Crissy

Within the same circus theme, three different carousels were created. One type was suspended from the ceiling and turned freely with the wooden bead bearings. String was used to thread the plastic bottle, bearings, and the carousel platform. Animals were later hung by thread from straw inserted into the platform.

Another carousel was made of wood, cardboard, and yarn. Animals were wound up backwards and released to revolve around the center. The momentum carried the horses into a clockwise and counter-clockwise canter. Each self-winding lost energy until the horses came to a standstill.

The last carousel was driven by a rubber band belt on two cotton reels, or spools. When turning a crank on one cotton reel, the second cotton reel had a corresponding movement. The carousel movement could be changed by turning the crank at different speeds and in either direction. The second cotton reel rotated an attached straw and cork platform from which the animals were suspended.

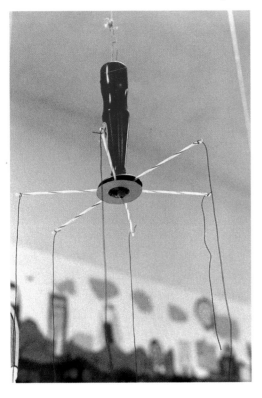

* * *

Angela's 6-year-olds dove into a challenge early in the school year. They had been fussing around with a photocopied spider pattern that, when folded properly, encircled a marble. As the marble rolled inside the spider, it moved down a ramp. Early discussions revealed further interest in this project. *How does it work? What are the most important parts? What critters could we make?*

The words "test", "modification" and "design" easily slipped into the children's working vocabulary, as Angela included these words in her exchanges with them. They found that the size and weight of their design could easily slow or stop the progress on the test ramp. Drag, or friction, played a big part in this difficulty. The children observed the movement of their critters and made adjustments that demonstrated an intuitive feeling for balance. They also swapped the original marble for a golf or tennis ball to correct inherent challenges of proportion. Some children found it necessary to place their "roller power" in a particular section of their design to make it move more quickly. They incorporated chambers into the design to contain the marble in that location. Children shared tales of the problems they faced and the solutions that were clearly theirs.

* * *

Susan and Rob read the story, *Wings: A Tale of Two Chickens*, to teachers of children ages 5-18. They encouraged them to listen for items in the tale that might be turned into three-dimensional models to be used in retelling the story. The teachers brainstormed a list of items central to the plot and characters. In order to create a workable number of possibilities, they combined and eliminated ideas based on the criteria of essential elements in the storyline, time, and available materials.

In discussing grouping strategies, the teachers generated two options: each group could develop models for the entire story or each group could develop one model for a collaborative retelling. Choosing the latter option, the teachers listed a variety of ways to move into working groups. They discussed the advantages of random grouping, grouping by friendship, groups based on complementary expertise, interest groups, and teacher-selected groups.

Given the challenge of integrating at least two engineering systems into their designs, groups were then identified and, before long, working teams were huddled over graph paper, work stations, and material caches. As they launched into the investigation phase, animated chatter and miming of movements were punctuated with spurts of "ahas". The groups explored movements and the engineering systems needed to achieve those movements, producing entanglements of arms and legs.

With great concentration, the fingers of one teacher became "pulleys" on which two other teachers tested their ideas for the motion of a particular pulley system they were trying to develop. One teacher pushed a swinging door several times in several places as he and his team members attempted to calculate where a syringe hydraulic system would be placed to gain the greatest leverage. Outstretched palms replicated the movement of alternating pistons driven by multiple cams. On the other side of the room, another team encountered a problem with wobbly pistons which moved the fox and pig up and down in the grocery store. Using fingers as a makeshift guide, the teacher team discovered the most effective placement for metal-rod guides and corrected the problem.

Teams created several versions of the lead character, a chicken. Other characters included a clever fox and a lively preacher. Several teachers constructed a geared fly swatter used to frighten away a cam-driven pest that bobbed up from an apple. Others produced a garden with alternating flower growth and a slot-guided sun. Possum Flats boasted the water tower, complete with a pneumatic escape system, where the lead character left a balloon. The grocery store was outfitted with a pulley-operated ladder and climbing grocer. Bells rang in the church tower, complete with tissue paper stained "glass", illuminated with electric light. Doors swung open powered by a hydraulic syringe. A motorized bicycle, made of soldered copper tubing, included a thumbtack-paperclip switch. A syringe-powered break-away cliff with sliding rocks fed straight into the mouth of a waiting sea monster. The motion of the monster's head and mouth were both controlled by hydraulics. Some groups took literary license to embellish the plot and add a personal touch to their interpretation. A hot air balloon swooped down on guide wires to rescue the dizzy chicken.

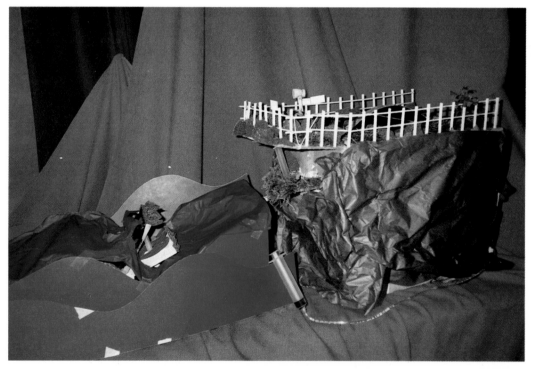

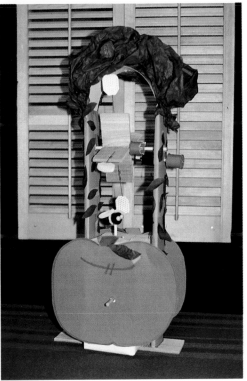

In celebration, the teachers retold the tale with spontaneous enthusiasm. Listening for the cue that called for their model, they sped to center stage to operate their creation as the narrators paused. They broke into applause in appreciation of the accomplishments, laughed at the delights produced by their afternoon's efforts, and shared the inner-workings of their designs. At the close of the session, teachers reflected on the challenges and successes of the day.

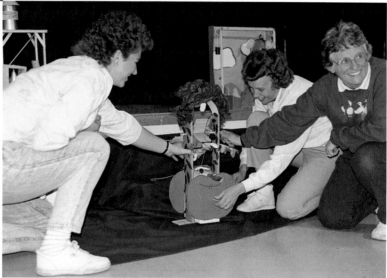

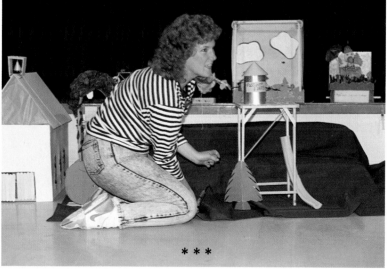

* * *

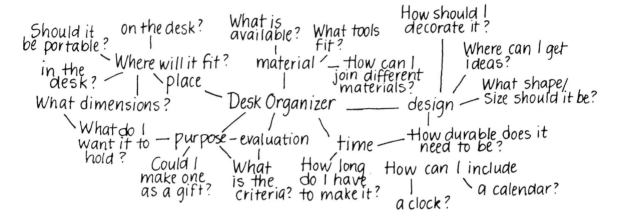

At the beginning of a school year, focusing on organization, middle school youngsters designed desk organizers to contain their supplies. Starting with a question web, the teacher modeled an organizational strategy for this and future planning. Children developed diverse prototypes from collections of plastic bottles, tin cans, cardboard tubes and boxes, and candy tins.

This allowed the teacher to observe the children in action. Baseline information was collected in the areas of cognitive, social, and physical development. She was able to ascertain approximate skill levels of each child, make note of their talents, and develop an initial learning agenda for needed skills and group work.

Early-year activities of this type provide teachers with initial information about their classes. *How do the children perceive and tackle challenges? How comfortable and successful are the children in collaborative learning? What organizational skills do the children possess?* The answers to these questions will shape the teacher's perspective from which she will design new experiences.

* * *

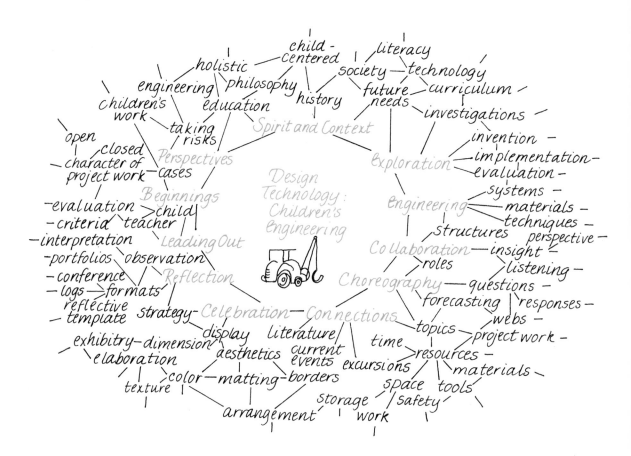

Perspectives

Design technology is a natural, intellectually, and physically interactive process of design, realization, and reflection. Through the consideration of ideas, aesthetics, implications, and available resources, children become imaginative engineers, exploring alternative solutions to contextualized challenges. Experiences in children's engineering, then, offer a complex web of interrelated skills and ideas; a dynamic instructional process necessary for unfound challenges of tomorrow.

As new opportunities in technology and education shape lifestyles of the next century, new perspectives are needed. A technological education of the future, in order to offer sound contributions to local and international concerns, calls for a synthesis of ideas and a dynamic paradigm for meaningful teaching and learning. This education is based upon needed technological skill as well as interactive learning which engages citizens in critical reflection and original thought.

Technological advances have increased in complexity and have moved beyond the scope of public understanding and management. Specialization, although necessary, when taken too far, limits the ability to find the connections among seemingly independent fields. Long-term effects of technological innovations, then, may be unknown and as a result, possess potential for unintended outcomes.

Historically, public access to science and technology has often been pursued through reductionistic avenues, breaking bodies of knowledge into fundamental parts. This well-intended approach produces highly abstract pieces of information, rather than a knowledge of essential interrelationships that exist. This may also produce dangerous and often detrimental social and scientific consequences of unforeseen patterns. Likewise, education has often followed reductionistic models of teaching and learning. Skills and sub-skills are enumerated as fundamental parts to be mastered. In isolation these skills remain abstract with little perceived connection or relevance. Children, in a world broken into fragmented and disconnected bits of information, struggle for meaning based on recall, rather than on the thoughtful integration and application of ideas. Recognition of connections will strengthen our ability to forecast, plan, and evaluate technological and educational advances.

It is characteristic of any research at the frontiers of knowledge that one never quite knows where it will lead, but, in the end, if everything goes well, one can often discern a consistent pattern of evolution in one's ideas and understanding.
Fritjof Capra, Uncommon Wisdom: Conversations with Remarkable People

---

Design technology integrates meaning in an instructional experience, with the child at the center. As an active investigator and sole inventor of personal meaning, the child is responsible for her own learning. In this child-centered approach, children are provided with opportunities to explore understanding of their world through contexts based upon their needs, capabilities, and desires. Similar to technological innovation, expressed human need is central to change and progress.

The teacher is able to work alongside the child to observe initial questions and intuitive beginnings, appreciate patterns of work, and reflect on what is known and how it is applied. In creating experiences that foster intrinsic motivation, the teacher becomes a resourcer and reflector, as well as a model and guide. Teaching and learning, then, become a process choreographed by inquisitive and dynamic minds.

Technology and education *can* acknowledge complexity, *can* become more personal, interactive and meaningful. This challenge is precipitated by the need to view technology and engineering as integrated, connected to the classroom curriculum. It encourages risk-taking in educational practice, not by *adding* engineering to the roster of mandatory subjects, but by *seeing* engineering *among* those subjects as a natural link. This approach to technological literacy is holistic by design and presents exciting futures in children's engineering.

Resources and Materials

The American Institute of Architects
Education Programs
1735 New York Avenue, N.W.
Washington, D.C.

Resource book, educational posters, and materials on design and architecture

American Society for Engineering Education
Suite 200 #11
Dupont Circle
Washington, D.C. 20036

Information and resources on engineering careers in the United States

The Design Council
28 Haymarket
London SW1Y 4SU
England

Publishers of THE BIG PAPER, a design technology resource paper, and additional resources in design and technology

E.J. Arnold & Sons Ltd..
Parkside Lane
Dewsbury Road
Leeds LS11 5TD
England

Suppliers of a wide range of educational equipment

EMA - Model Supplies, Ltd.
58 - 60 The Centre
Feltham TW13 4BH
England

Materials and supplies for children's engineering

Junior Engineering Technical Society (JETS)
1420 King Street #405
Alexandria, Virginia 22314-2715

Teacher and student resources and programs for middle school and high school. Inquiries should include a stamped self-addressed envelope.

Lego Systems, Inc.
555 Taylor Road
Enfield, CT 06082-3298

Manipulatives for teaching science, math, and engineering using computer control systems, an interface box, and LEGO ™
Suppliers of LEGO products and accredited training

National Academy of Engineering
2101 Constitution Avenue, N.W.
Washington, D.C. 20418

National organization of engineers sponsoring programs in engineering education and research at the college level

Oregon Museum of Science and Industry
4015 S.W. Canyon Road
Portland, Oregon 97221

Design technology tools, supplies, resource books, and workshops for teachers

Plastruct
1020 S. Wallace Place
City of Industry, California 91748-1087

Model and craft supplies for children's engineering

Technology Teaching Systems
Penmore House, Hasland Road
Hasland, Chesterfield S41 OSJ
England

Classroom teaching materials for primary schools

End Notes

Foreword

John Dewey in de Lima, Agnes *et al.* (1942) p.*x*.

Spirit and Context

For further descriptions of constructivism, a view of cognitive development, see Bybee, R. and Sund, R. (1982); Ginsburg, H. and Opper, S. (1969); Foreman, G. and Kuschner, D. (1983); Rebok, G. (1987); Kamii, C. and DeVries, R. (1978) and Kegan, R. (1982).

The Design Council (1987) section 4.2.

Dewey, J. (1938) p. 47.

Wenk, E. (1986) pp. 2 and 18.

Rebok, G. (1987) p. 26.

For a detailed history of reductionism in science and holistic paradigms in science learning see Capra, F. (1982) and (1988).

Perspectives on science, engineering, technology and society are given considerable attention in Bybee, R. (Ed.) (1986); Wenk, E. (1986); Schumacher, E. (1973); Shapley, D. and Roy, R. (1985); National Academy of Engineering (1988); US Congress, Office of Technology Assessment (1988) and the American Association for the Advancement of Science (1989).

Exploration

Additional perspectives and discussion of the design technology process are found in Department of Education and Science (1982).

Comprehensive discussion of holographic theory is found in Ferguson, M. (1980) and Wilber, K. (Ed.) (1982).

Williams, P. and Jinks, D. (1985) p. 38.

Harlen, W. (1985) p. *xi*.

Distinctions among types of curriculum are described in Glatthorn, A. (1987).

Discussion of science goals and teaching for children ages 5 - 13 is found in Ennever, L. and Harlen, W. (1972)(1985) and (1987); Osborne, R. and Freyburg, P. (1985) and Carin, A. and Sund, R. (1985).

Department of Education and Science (1982) p. 84.

For additional thoughts on children's learning of mathematics see Kazuko Kamii, C. with DeClark, G. (1985) and Baroody, A. (1987).

Further insights into language use and writing are found in McCormick Calkins, L. (1983); Fulwiler, T. (Ed.) (1987); Graves, D. (1983); Hanson, J. *et al.* (1985); Holdaway, D. (1979); Edwards, A.D. and Westgate, D.P.G. (1987) and Newman, J. (1985).

Loughlin, C. and Suina, J. (1982) p. 105.

Art and craft techniques may be found in Cunningham-Craig, J. and Ammond, J. (Eds) (1988) and Good, K. (1987).

Lancaster, J. (Ed.) (1987) p. 7.

Engineering

We extend our appreciation to Vicki Nebel, Gary Isaacson and Randy Lakey for sharing children's work from Redland School.

For specific techniques for drawing, structures, connectors, and application of systems and energy sources, refer to Williams, P. and Jinks, D. (1985); Breckon, A. and Prest, D. (1987); Toft, P. (1987); Good, K. (1987); Aitken, J. and Mills, G. (1987) and Dunn, S. (1986).

For strategies in drawing, design, thinking and problem-solving, see Hanks, K. *et al.* (1977).

Collaboration

For research on cooperative learning in science education, see Johnson, R. and Johnson, D. (1987).

Examples of teacher-child dialogue may be found in Ennever, L. and Harlen, W. (1972).

Ferguson, M. (1980) p. 292.

Wray, D. (1988) p. 46.

American Association for the Advancement of Science (1989) p. 148.

Choreography

Inquiry strategies are discussed in Joyce, B. and Weil, M. (1986) and Orlich, D. *et al.* (1985).

Ferguson, M. (1980) p. 292.

Wray, D. (1988) p. 38

Discussion of tools and more information about materials science, the characteristics and use of materials, is found in Good, K. (1987); Breckon, A. and Prest, D. (1987); Toft, P. (1987) and Dunn, S. (1986).

Loughlin, C. and Suina, J. (1982) p. 106.

Useful ideas and considerations for planning classroom environments are found in Kritchevsky, S. and Prescott, E. with Walling, L. (1977) and Loughlin, C. and Suina, J. (1982).

We thank Jo Rossman of the Beaverton School District for the use of excerpts from her parent letter.

Connections

We extend our appreciation to the following teachers for allowing us to use examples of their plans and children's work: Bill Noomah, Susan Larfield, Sherie Hildreth, Cathy Griswold, Judi Gettel, Lori Buchanan, Stephanie Buzbee, Nancy Jensen and Gail Rupp.

Approaches to themes and project work are outlined in Wray, D. (1988); Tann, C.S. (1988) and Kerry, T. and Eggleston, J. (1988).

Capra, F. (1988) p. 20.

Raven, A. (1987) p. 2.

Dewey, J. (1938) p. 80.

Duckworth, E. (1972) p. 231.

Schiller, C., found in Griffin-Beale, C. (1979).

Celebration

We thank Donna Bauer, Don Werner, Scott Mulligan and John Allgood for examples of their work that appear in this chapter.

Display techniques are set forth in Greenstreet, D. (1985).

ILEA (Inner London Education Authority) Teachers' Art Centre, found in Greenstreet, D. (1985) p. 3.

Reflection

Ferguson, M. (1980) p. 292.

Information about the Department of Education and Science assessment scheme in design technology is presented in Kelly *et al.* (1987).

Activities and investigation in the exploration and analysis of design components may be found in Perkins, D. and Laserna, C. (1986) and Perkins, D. (1986).

Leading Out

Beginnings

We thank the following teachers for allowing us to share their classroom experiences as examples of good practice: Judy Holmes, Sid Caba, Sharon Greenfield, Helen Crowell, Patty Beauchamp, Helen Nolen-Balduchi, Connie Larson, Barbara Eichelberger, Jim Adams, Mary Kilmer, Jennifer Kerr, Angela Loveall and Jennifer Herrick.

Spurr, E. (1985) *Mrs Minnetta's Carpool,* New York: Atheneum.

Schiller, C., found in Griffin-Beale, C. (1979) p. 92.

Marshall, J. (1986) *Wings: A Tale of Two Chickens*, New York: Viking Kestrel.

Perspectives

Capra, F. (1988) p. 12.

We also express our appreciation to the following educators for their contributions to our work: Ashley Ross, David Argles, Monika Choudhury, Keith Good, Michele Brenner, JoAnn Fordyce, Francis Brady, Janice Leonetti and Steve Thompson.

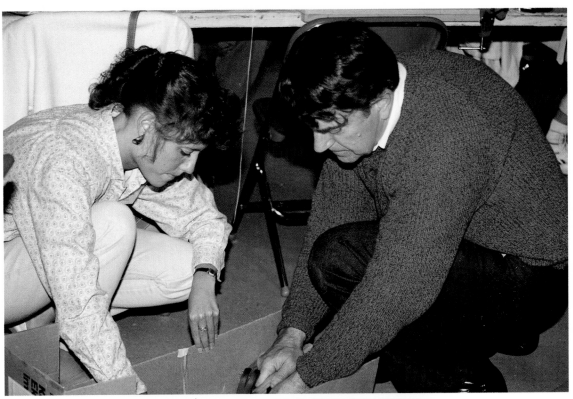

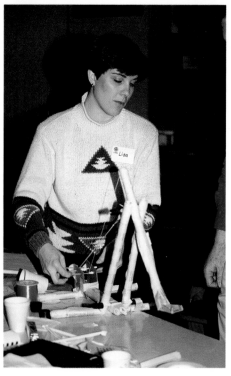

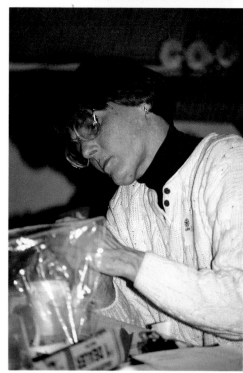

Bibliography

Aitken, John and Mills, George (1987) *Creative Technology: A Class-room Resource,* New York: Holmes McDougal.

American Association for the Advancement of Science (AAAS) (1989) *Science for All Americans: A Project 2061 Report on Literacy Goals in Science, Mathematics and Technology,* Washington DC: AAAS.

Baroody, Arthur (1987) *Children's Mathematical Thinking: A Developmental Framework for Preschool, Primary and Special Education Teachers,* New York: Columbia Teachers Press.

Breckon, Andrew and Prest, David (1987) *Introducing Craft, Design and Technology,* London: Hutchinson.

Bybee, Rodger (Ed.) (1986) *Science Technology Society, NSTA Yearbook 1985,* Washington DC: National Science Teachers Association.

Bybee, Rodger and Sund, Robert (1982) *Piaget for Educators,* Columbus OH: Charles E. Merrill.

Capra, Fritjoh (1982) *The Turning Point,* New York: Bantam Books.

Capra, Fritjoh (1988) *Uncommon Wisdom: Conversations with Remarkable People,* New York: Bantam Books.

Carin, Arthur and Sund, Robert (1985) *Teaching Science through Discovery,* Columbus OH: Bell and Howell.

Cunningham-Craig, Jackie and Hammond, Jane (Eds) (1988) *Teacher Handbooks: Art and Craft Techniques,* Leamington Spa: Scholastic.

Department of Education and Science (1982a) *Understanding Design and Technology* (Assessment of Performance Unit discussion draft), London: HMSO.

Department of Education and Science (1982b) *Mathematics Counts* (The Cockcroft Report), London: HMSO.

Design Council (1987) *Design and Primary Education: The Report of the Design Council's Primary Education Working Party,* London, The Design Council.

Dewey, John (1938) *Experience and Education*, New York: Macmillan.

Duckworth, Eleanor (1972) 'The having of wonderful ideas', *Harvard Educational Review*, **42**, pp. 217-31.

Dunn, Stewart (1986) *An Introduction to Craft Design Technology*, London: Bell and Hyman.

Edwards, Anthony and Westgate, David (1987) *Investigating Classroom Talk*, Lewes: Falmer Press.

Ennever, Len *et al.* (1972) *With Objectives in Mind* (Schools Council Publications), London: McDonald.

Ferguson, Marilyn (1980) *The Aquarian Conspiracy: Personal and Social Transformation in the 1980s*, Los Angeles, CA: J.P. Tarcher.

Forman, George and Kuschner, David (1983) *The Child's Construction of Knowledge: Piaget for Teaching Children*, Washington DC: National Association for the Education of Young Children.

Fulwiler, Toby (Ed.) (1987) *The Journal Book*, Portsmouth NH: Boynton/Cook Publishers.

Ginsburg Herbert and Opper, Sylvia (1969) *Piaget's Theory of Intellectual Development*, Englewood Cliffs NJ: Prentice Hall.

Glatthorn, Allan, A. (1987) *Curriculum Renewal*, Alexandria VA: Association for Supervision and Curriculum Development.

Good, Keith (1987) *Starting CDT*, London: Heinemann.

Graves, Donald (1983) *Writing: Teachers and Children at Work*, Portsmouth NH: Heinemann.

Greenstreet, Derek (1985) *Ways to Display*, London: Ward Lock Educational.

Griffin-Beale, Christopher (Ed.) (1979) *Christian Schiller: In His Own Words*, London: A&C Black.

Hans, Kurt *et al.* (1977) *Design Yourself*, Los Altos CA: William Kaufmann.

Hanson, Jane, NewKirk, Thomas and Graves, Donald (Eds) (1985) *Breaking Ground: Teachers Relate Reading and Writing in the Elementary School*, Portsmouth NH: Heinemann.

Harlen, Wynne (1985) *Teaching and Learning Primary Science*, London: Harper and Row.

Harlen, Wynne (Ed.) (1987) *Primary Science: Taking the Plunge*, London: Heinemann.

Holdaway, Don (1979) *The Foundations of Literacy*, Gosford NSW: Ashton Scholastic.

Johnson, Roger and Johnson, David (1987) 'Cooperative learning and the achievement and socialization crises in science and mathematics classrooms', in **Champagne, A. and Hornig, R.** (Eds) *Students and Science Learning, Papers from the 1987 National Forum for School Science*, Washington DC: AAAS.

Joyce, Bruce and Weil, Marsha (1986) *Models of Teaching*, Englewood Cliffs NJ: Prentice Hall.

Kamii, Constance and DeVries, Rheta (1978) *Physical Knowledge in Preschool Education: Implications of Piaget's Theory*, Englewood Cliffs NJ: Prentice Hall.

Kazuko Kamii, Constance with DeClark, Georgia (1985) *Young Children Reinvent Arithmetic: Implications of Piaget's Theory*, New York: Teachers College Press.

Kegan, Robert (1982) *The Evolving Self: Problem and Process in Human Development*, Cambridge MA: Harvard University Press.

Kelly, A. *et al.* (1987) *Design and Technology Activity: A Fremwork for Assessment* (Assessment of Performance Unit), London: HMSO.

Kerry, Trevor and Eggleston, Jim (1988) *Topic Work in the Primary School*, London: Routledge.

Kritchevsky, Sybil and Prescott, Elizabeth with Walling, Lee (1977) *Planning Environments for Young Children: Physical Space* (2nd edn), Washington DC: National Association for the Education of Young Children.

Lancaster, John (Ed.) (1987) *Art, Craft and Design in the Primary School*, Corsham: National Society for Education in Art and Design.

de Lima, Agnes *et al.* (1942) *The Little Red Schoolhouse*, New York: Macmillan.

Loughlin, Catherine and Suina, Joseph (1982) *The Learning Environment: An Instructional Strategy*, New York: Teachers College Press.

McCormick Calkins, Lucy (1983) *Lessons from a Child: On the Teaching and Learning of Writing*, Portsmouth NH: Heinemann.

National Academy of Engineering (1988) *Focus of the Future: A National Action Plan for Career-long Education for Engineers,* Washington DC: National Academy of Engineering.

Newman, Judith (1985) *Whole Language: Theory in Use,* Portsmouth NH: Heinemann.

Osborne, Roger and Freyberg, Peter (1985) *Learning in Science: The Implications of Children's Science,* Auckland, Heinemann.

Orlich, Donald *et al.* (1985) *Teaching Strategies: A Guide to Better Instruction,* Lexington MA: D.C. Heath.

Perkins, David (1986) *Knowledge as Design,* Hillsdale NJ: Lawrence Erlbaum.

Perkins, David and Laserna Catalina (1986) *Inventive Thinking* (Odyssey: A Curriculum for Thinking series) Watertown MA: Mastery Education.

Raven, Andrew (1987) unpublished manuscript.

Rebok, George W. (1987) *Life-span Cognitive Development,* New York: Holt, Rinehart and Winston.

Schumacher, E.F. (1973) *Small is Beautiful: A Study of Economics as if People Mattered,* London: Abacus.

Shapley, Deborah and Roy, Rustum (1985) *Lost at the Frontier,* Philadelphia PA: ISI Press.

Tann, C. Sarah (Ed.) (1988) *Developing Topic Work in the Primary School,* Lewes: Falmer Press.

Toft, Peter (1987) *CDT for GCSE,* London: Heinemann.

US Congress, Office of Technology Assessment (1988) *Educating Scientists and Engineers: Grade School to Grad School* (OTA-SET-377), Washington DC: US Government Printing Office.

Wenk, Edward (1986) *Tradeoffs: Imperatives of Choice in a High-tech World,* Baltimore MD: Johns Hopkins University Press.

Wilber, Ken (Ed.) (1982) *The Holographic Paradigm and other Paradoxes. Exploring the Leading Edge of Science,* Boulder CO: Shambhala.

Williams, Pat and Jinks, David (1985) *Design & Technology: 5 - 12,* Lewes: Falmer Press.

Wray, D. (1988) *Project Teaching,* Leamington Spa: Scholastic.